THE TRUMP SECRET

Seeing Through the Past, Present, and Future of the New American President

RYUHO OKAWA

IRH Press

The material in this book is selected from various talks given by Ryuho Okawa to a live audience.

BOOKS
IRH PRESS
New York

Library of Congress Cataloging-in-Publication Data

ISBN 13: 978-1-942125-22-8
ISBN 10: 1-942125-22-4

Printed in Canada

First edition

Cover Designer: Whitney Cookman

*No statements made by the guardian spirit of Donald Trump in this book reflect statements actually made by Donald Trump himself.

CONTENTS

PUBLISHER'S INTRODUCTION ... 9

Part I

Chapter 1

On VICTORY *of* MR. DONALD TRUMP

Realizing Prosperity and Justice in America and the World

Preface for Chapter 1 21

1. Guardian Spirit Already Said, "I Will Be the Next President" in January of this Year 22
2. His Victory Comes from His Strategy and God's Wind From Heaven 24
3. Trump Will End the Conflict in Middle East 26
4. He is the President of 'Wisdom and Courage' 28
5. Economic Strategy Against China 30
6. Two Sides of Trump: Economic Thinking and World Justice 33
7. America Should Play the Role of World Policeman Again ... 35

Question 1 36

Question 2 41

Question 3 47

CHAPTER 2

FREEDOM, JUSTICE, *and* HAPPINESS

Preface for Chapter 2 55

1. New York is a Little Different from Eight Years Ago 56
2. America has the Mission to Make a New Dream for the World 58
3. Be the "United States of America," not the "Divided States of America" 60
4. The Growing Crisis of Asia 62
5. A New Philosophy from the U.S.A. to the World 64
6. Leaders of the World Need God's View 66
7. America, Be Greater 67

Question 1 69

Question 2 74

Part II

Chapter 3

SPIRITUAL INTERVIEW *with* GEORGE WASHINGTON

Revealing Donald Trump's Hidden Identity

Preface for Chapter 3 81

1. America's Founding Father Washington Appears 84
2. In the American Presidential Election, He Supports the "Honest Man" 87
3. On Racial Problems in Current America 96
4. He Helped God Make a New Civilization 101
5. On America's Foreign Policies on the Middle East and Russia 104
6. On American and World Economies 106
7. On Problems with North Korea 110
8. The Secret of the God of America 113
9. His Past Lives as a God in India, Europe, and Africa ... 119
10. Declaring His Rebirth as Donald Trump 122

CHAPTER 4

THE TRUMP CARD *in the* UNITED STATES

Spiritual Messages from the Guardian Spirit of Donald Trump

Preface for Chapter 4 129

1. The Guardian Spirit of "The Next President" Trump Appears 132
2. The True Intention in the Violent Remarks Against Immigrants 136
3. On the Criticisms from the Mass Media 142
4. Being Honest Appears as Discrimination Against Women 147
5. Views On Japan-U.S. Ties, Japan-South Korea Ties, Russia, Iran and China 151
6. What Would Hillary Bring as the President? 158
7. Recovering the U.S. Economy 162
8. Expectations for the Muslim Immigrants in the U.S. ... 169
9. Form a Triangle of God-Believing Countries and Stand Against Atheist China 172
10. A "Big Name" from Trump's Past Lives 176
11. Message for the Prosperity of Japan and the U.S. 182

About the Author 187
What is a Spiritual Message? 190
About Happy Science 194
Contact Information 196
Happiness Realization Party 199
Happy Science University 200
About IRH Press USA Inc. 202
Books by Ryuho Okawa 203
Movies 208

PUBLISHER'S INTRODUCTION

The 2016 United States election shocked the world. United States pollsters, the international media and laymen from all political affiliations never expected a political novice to handily defeat a roster of career politicians in the primaries and then shut down the hopes of Hillary Clinton becoming the first female United States President.

But one person who was not surprised by Donald Trump's victory was Ryuho Okawa, the Global Visionary, a renowned spiritual leader, and international best-selling author. Okawa had foreseen and predicted Trump's victory speaking publicly on January 5, 2016 about his vision that Donald Trump would win the United States election with a non traditional plan, thereby defeating two American political dynasties—Bush and Clinton.

The Trump Secret: Seeing Through the Past, Present, and Future of the New American President, shows businessman Trump's creative path to the American Presidency and forecasts how he will approach unifying America, strengthening a worsening world economy, and interacting with friends and adversaries alike, and how he will utilize a unique style not seen since the days of George Washington.

Ryuho Okawa has been observing United States politics, its economy, and its changing posture in the international community since the mid 1980s when he worked on Wall Street. While he is a Japanese religious leader, he has been making his opinion clear in fields beyond religious matters—Japanese and international politics, economics, education, science, and more.

He has given over 2,500 lectures (each with different content) and has written over 2,100 titles. While being a national teacher in Japan, he has been increasing impact on a worldwide level, both through live broadcasts and TV programs, in addition to publication of his translated books. In 2016, he appeared on TV Sunday mornings on the Fox affiliate in New York City and appeared in *The National Review*, *The Weekly Standard*, and *The Economist* among other publications.

In 2014, Okawa wrote *Into the Storm of International Politics: The New Standards of the World Order* and criticized the Obama Administration for abdicating its role as the world's policeman and opening up the vacuums in the Middle East that were filled by the Islamic State and Russia and allowing the rogue regime in North Korea to further develop nuclear weapons and the Chinese government to consolidate economic and military power.

In 2016, Okawa authored *The Laws of Justice: How We Can Solve World Conflicts and Bring Peace* focusing on international terrorism, the rise of ISIS, the Syrian Civil War and the refugee crisis, the military expansion of China and nuclear development by North Korea. This book navigates world leaders, academic thinkers, and thoughtful readers to best analyze how they can reach Okawa's ultimate goal: to help people find true happiness and bring justice and prosperity to the world.

Okawa also analyzes the two major trends opposing each other in the world—one force comprised of countries that want to support and spread the ideologies of democracy, liberty, fundamental human rights and market economies, and the other is a force of the countries that will suffer if these ideologies spread across the world, because their way of thinking and methods differ.

In his hundreds of spiritual interviews, Okawa has communicated the words of present and past leaders around the world, including Barack Obama, Hillary Clinton, Vladimir Putin, Xi Jinping, and Kim Jong-un to name a few*. In addition to predicting the 2016 American election months in advance, Okawa predicted in December 1990 the Britain's exit from the EU and also in February 2014, how the South Korean people would bring down President Park Geun-hye†.

---

*Okawa employs his psychic ability to conduct spiritual interviews with the guardian spirit, or consciousness, of a person—this new type of interview is already acknowledged in many countries. These spiritual interviews represent the thoughts, ideas and beliefs of those interviewed and not those of Ryuho Okawa or of Happy Science Group.

† See Ryuho Okawa, *Why I am Anti-Japan: Interviewing the Guardian Spirit of Korean President Park Geun-hye* [Tokyo: HS Press, 2014].

During the 8 years of the Obama Administration, the United States has gone through changes that Okawa sees as the catalyst of the stunning election that had Trump win over the working class voters in blue states such as Michigan, Wisconsin, and Pennsylvania.

On the domestic level, Okawa recognizes that the growth of America's GDP has been waning at 1.8 percent. The United States regulation code grew in 2016 from 80,000 pages to 90,000 pages. The United States tax code has ballooned to 2.8 million words and needs 7.7 million words to explain it. This economic catastrophe does not include the burgeoning entitlements and the failure of ObamaCare.

Since 2008, Obama had lost for the Democrats 13 Senate seats, 69 House seats, 11 Governorships, and 30 legislatures have turned from Democrat to Republican (as of November 2016). These facts support Okawa's early evaluation that Donald Trump would lead a populist revolution.

In Chapter 1 of *The Trump Secret: Seeing Through the Past, Present, and Future of the New American President*, Ryuho Okawa spoke in Japan the day after the American election. He forecasts what will happen as a result of Trump's victory, including how the Middle East conflict will turn out, economic strategies the U.S. will wage against China, Trump's plans to address illegal immigration and terrorism, proposed tax policies, and America's future relations with

Russia. Calling Trump's mouth "the new weapon for new age," Okawa acknowledges that it can sound "radical and extreme," but it's time "America should be strong."

He argues that this is America's last opportunity to rebalance world powers based on the Obama administration's "tendency of withdrawing and declining," which "made the world more complicated" including Russian relations, the Syrian conflict, and absent North Korean policy. Despite the media criticism, Okawa in his speech calls Trump "intelligent" and believes he has "wisdom" and "courage." Okawa predicts that Trump will rebuild the American economy, have hegemony in foreign affairs, and remake the relationship with Russia. He forecasts that "the relationship between Putin and Trump will change the relationship between China and Japan, China and Russia, and China and North Korea." Okawa believes that Trump "is a very moderate person and he has a very soft touch."

Chapter 2 is based on Okawa's public talk given in New York City on October 2, 2016. This chapter is Okawa's empowering and encouraging message to the people of the United States. He calls on Americans to become aware of America's role as the world leader once again so that we can together achieve freedom, justice, and happiness. After viewing New York City, Okawa comments how he saw a silence, a lack of vitality, and no philosophy.

He calls on the United States not to be "the Divided States of America. Be America the United States. Red States and Blue States should aim at the end to the same goal." Saying that Americans with upper-level income have decreased in number, and the bottom level had diminished leaving a larger middle class, he states Obama has prompted an America that "has the tendency of hating or envy for wealthy people." He warns, "If the United States of America hesitates to let people be wealthy, it will lead to the end of America." He implores Americans to fulfill "the mission to make a new American dream for the world" and that they "must think that the citizens of the United States are not American" but they "are the world citizen, the world leader."

The final two chapters represent Ryuho Okawa's spiritual interviews with George Washington and Donald Trump. Chapter 3 is based on an interview session recorded in September 2016. In this interview, George Washington speaks through Okawa and answers questions on the 2016 U.S. presidential election, evaluates the eight years of Obama administration, and tells his vision of America in the 21st century.

This interview shows that Trump's radical statements are reminiscent of how George Washington operated and foreshadows that a Trump Presidency may resemble Washington and shake America on its 240th birthday.

Chapter 4 unveils Donald Trump's subconscious thoughts, or his honest feelings and intentions, about various issues including illegal immigration, media's criticisms against him, Chinese expansionism, his plans to "make America great again," and relations with Japan, China, South Korea, Russia, and Islamic countries. In the interview, Trump's guardian spirit states, "Criticism is... a sweet dessert for me. When you want a cup of coffee, you want some cake or something like that, right? For me, criticism is a New York cheesecake." His guardian spirit adds, "Every criticism will be advertising for me because I'm strong. I am confident of my ability."

The Trump Secret: Seeing Through the Past, Present, and Future of the New American President continues to establish Okawa as an extraordinary powerful thinker and teacher who views and interprets domestic politics, international relations, and the economy from academic, practical, spiritual, and religious perspectives. It provides great optimism about America's future as Okawa gives readers a glimpse of his vision that laymen and world leaders alike have awaited for years.

PART I

CHAPTER 1

On VICTORY *of* MR. DONALD TRUMP

Realizing Prosperity and Justice in America and the World

Held November 10, 2016
Happy Science General Headquarters, Tokyo

This lecture was held a day after the results of the presidential election was released.

This is "what I believe."

America is still alive.

America should be America.

America should be a great and strong teacher.

The result shows God's will.

Now is the time to believe.

The victory of Mr. Donald Trump is the answer.

He will rebuild the United States greater again.

I hope so. We hope so. People of the world hope so.

This is the correct answer.

America shall not be divided again.

Ryuho Okawa
Master and CEO of Happy Science Group
November 11, 2016

From the Preface given for the book, Trump Shindaitoryo de Sekai wa Ko Ugoku [*On Victory of Mr. Donald Trump*] (*Tokyo: IRH Press, 2016*).

1

GUARDIAN SPIRIT ALREADY SAID, "I WILL BE THE NEXT PRESIDENT" IN JANUARY OF THIS YEAR

Yesterday [November 9, 2016], we recognized the conclusion of the presidential race of the United States, and as you know, Donald Trump won. It's very happy for us because we did "a little" for Mr. Trump. My cuffs button, this is not so precious one, but he gave me these cuffs in respect for my New York mission.* So, I appreciated him and he also appreciated me. We are Avengers†, so we can respect each other.

Early this year, in January, I published the spiritual message from the guardian spirit of Donald Trump‡ [see Chapter 4]. In that book, he already said, "I'm not the frontrunner of the presidency. I will be the next

* On October 2nd, 2016, Master Ryuho Okawa gave a lecture in English, "Freedom, Justice, and Happiness" at Crowne Plaza Times Square Manhattan in New York. Included as Chapter 2 in this book.

† A piece featuring a team of various American comic book heroes. A film was made in 2012 which was considered a big hit, and a sequel was released in 2015.

‡ Ryuho Okawa, *Shugorei Interview Donald Trump America Fukkatsueno Senryaku* [Spiritual Interview with the Guardian Spirit of Donald Trump - The Strategy to Rebuild the United States] (Tokyo: IRH Press, 2016). Included as Chapter 4 in this book. For more on spiritual message and guardian spirit, see end section.

president." He repeatedly said so. And this was not a joke. He became president, as you know. This is his confidence, I think so.

But at the time, audience might have thought that it was his joke because he said at the time that he's the rebirth of George Washington, the founder of the United States and he said, "I will be the next president." So, the audience might have felt that he's just joking, or as always, he said that he talks a lot about him, bigger than he is.

But in reality, he said the truth and in that conversation, our Miss Isis Mariko talked about him that he's an honest man and he thought that it's very suitable for him. And I visited this October and gave a lecture at New York's hotel and I repeatedly said he's an honest man and reliable man and responsible man. This is my honest opinion of him.

2

HIS VICTORY COMES FROM HIS STRATEGY AND GOD'S WIND FROM HEAVEN

To tell the truth, American mass media and Japanese mass media and, of course, a lot of intelligent people who can speak a lot about him by writing or by speaking through the media didn't think his victory. But I continuously insisted that he deserves to be the next president. He has such kind of capacity and reliability as the next president of the United States. But American scholars and journalists couldn't understand what I said because Donald Trump is very difficult to understand from the outside.

He, himself, has new weapon for new age. This is the weapon through his mouth, I mean, the radical words, radical and creative words. Sometimes it sounds very extreme, and sometimes he was told that he is accustomed to make sexual harassment or racial harassment, like that. But I think that he indeed is a gentleman and he sometimes acts like Mr. Duterte of the Philippines, but in reality, he is not such kind of type. He is a very intelligent and wise person, and he has calculations for the reaction of the mass media.

And I guessed that he will win, this summer, because Mr. Trump let the media dance at his will. When we read newspapers from America or we watched TV of the American news, Mr. Trump appeared twice as many times as Ms. Clinton. It is a strategy, I think so. He is very wise, clever. His money for running the presidency was smaller than Ms. Clinton's money and also, his moving mates for presidency had been fewer than Hillary's. But he finally won.

In reality, when we watched the TV yesterday, we felt some kind of so-called kamikaze, the wind of god, from Heaven. The real difference of the number of the votes is about one million or so*. Of course, Mr. Trump won against Ms. Clinton, but almost one million. But he got a great victory. It comes from his strategy, I think so. People of the world know Donald Trump very much in this year. His strategy of the propaganda was very systematic and reasonable.

So, it's a very good sample even for us in Japan to deal with political activity of Japan. If the mass media predict the result of the election, it always holds true.

---

*As of December 3, Trump had approximately 62.8 million votes and Clinton, 65.4 million.

But in America, as you just watched several or ten or more hours ago, the result could change.

I think this is one aspect of democracy. People who have the right for voting can choose by their own, or his own or her own, thinking. Just on their own mind, not on the tendency of the mass media or intelligent people or casters or famous scholars. They hear from them, but they judge by themselves and they change their mind in these two or three days, I guess so. This is, from one aspect is, kamikaze, the god's wind. I have been blowing God's wind from Heaven, so that several million people would change their mind through these two or three days.

3

TRUMP WILL END THE CONFLICT IN MIDDLE EAST

And in addition to that, we, Happy Science, especially the members of the USA, acted politically. It might be the first experience for them. We are a religion born in Japan and usually counted as the minority-type of religion and, of course, our American members support the Democrats rather than the Republicans usually because they are requiring the equal rights for White-American, WASP people.

But this time, I predicted that now, it's time for strong president or it's time America should be America, America should be stronger. It's the last chance for them to make rebalance between the world powers because during the presidency of Mr. Barack Obama and these eight years, he has a tendency of withdrawing and declining. So, it's made the world more complicated.

For example, the trouble of the Syria and Iraq, I mean the IS. If there were not Mr. Obama and Mrs. Clinton, at that time, there would be no IS now. Mr. Obama's lure for peaceful world or Nobel Prize-like peaceful world caused the next turbulence in Iraq and Syria. There appeared ISIS and they are battling now. Donald Trump may cease the fire because he has such kind of ability and judgment and capability.

And Mr. Obama's great failure was his misunderstanding for Russia. He made the worst relationship between Russia and the United States. It's made quite opposite to his rebalance policy. It makes the world balance worse and worse. It makes Russia alone and lets

Russia close to China.

Mr. Obama and Mrs. Clinton did nothing for the North Korean policy. They just pushed Beijing, I mean the People's Republic of China. But in reality, it means their weakness, I think so. If the president were Bush Jr., North Korea couldn't do such rude deeds again and again.

4

HE IS THE PRESIDENT OF 'WISDOM AND COURAGE'

So, Mr. Trump should learn a lot from today. But I think his intelligence is enough. He is the president of wisdom and courage. Wisdom and courage are most suitable for the forty-fifth president of the United States. They need wisdom.

Barack Obama is a clever person, but he doesn't have enough wisdom, I think so. Hillary also. But Mr. Trump has wisdom and he also has courage. TV reporters of Japan say that Beijing, I mean Xi Jinping, thinks that Hillary would be more difficult to deal with than Donald Trump, and Donald Trump is easy for them to deal with. But I think it's very contrary.

Hillary is the extension of Barack Obama's foreign policy, but Donald Trump would change their diplomatic policy because he is a thinkable man. And he will think of the foreign policy from scratch. He thinks of the world balance from the standpoint of equal-ness and fairness. That is my impression.

People of the world, especially Japanese foreign ministry or government, are just worrying about TPP or Trans-Pacific Partnership treaty. Of course, Donald Trump and Hillary Clinton both declared refusal to join the treaty, but we must think about this seriously, deeply.

5

ECONOMIC STRATEGY AGAINST CHINA

Donald Trump thinks that the tariff system, I mean the import tax system, is one of the weapons for diplomacy. He thinks so. It means, for example, he can use high tax rate for China if he doesn't like their foreign policy. For example, China wants to intrude some kind of Asian country. He will change the tax rate for China, the import tax rate for China. It is one of the weapons without hot war, without bullet, without missile, without the seventh fleet. He is just thinking this point.

I already said that the TPP is important for Japan because it was created as the counter power of the AIIB* of China. AIIB is the foreign policy which will make China the leader of the world, so we need the Trans-Pacific Partnership and no higher tax barrier regarding the Pacific Rim.

It is Obama's thinking. Japan must join this policy. If not, China will win in foreign diplomacy and trad-

* Asia Infrastructure Investment Bank is a multilateral development bank for the Asian region. China took the initiative in establishing this institution in Dec. 2015, with 57 member states as its Founding Members.

ing diplomacy with Africa and west part of Asia, and of course the north, south and east parts of Asia. And they can dispel the United States to Hawaii. This is their basic doctrine. So, we need TPP.

But Mr. Trump will rethink about this. Of course, Mr. Obama will persuade Donald Trump that he should join the TPP and the Japanese government is in a hurry to pass this alignment to the TPP. And before the retirement of Barack Obama, Japan will make a pressure to the United States to join this TPP before Mr. Trump takes office in the White House.

But now, at this point, we must think we have two ways. Of course, one is to join the TPP and guard the Transpacific trade and make prosperity, and another one is as Donald Trump said, "Make America greater again" and have new leadership for the world.

At this point, he said America is not the world's policeman, like Obama said, but it's not his real thinking, I think so. He will firstly rebuild the American economy and next, he will have hegemony in foreign affairs and in addition to that, he will want to remake the relationship between Russia and America.

Of course, he insisted that Japan should be Japan. He said so. I think this is truth and this is justice. Japan should be Japan. Japan is the world's second or third largest economic country. I said the second or the third; it means China's economic statistics is not believable. So, they have some kind of bubbly figures in their economic plan.

For example, they said that this year, the economic growth is 6.7 percent each quarter. It's a national growth planning rate; just the same rate. It's impossible in the real economy. The figure is very controlled for and they (Chinese communist officials) don't want to be fired by Xi Jinping, so we cannot rely on them. In reality, the real economy is not so different from, in conclusion, I mean Chinese and Japanese economic growth and power are not so different, I think so. It will be revealed in the near two or three years, I think so.

6

TWO SIDES OF TRUMP: ECONOMIC THINKING AND WORLD JUSTICE

And Mr. Trump will insist that, as you know, Japanese mass media are upset by his saying that "Japan has a nuclear power" or "Japan is too big to protect. Japan should protect herself." He said so.

In reality, in the standpoint of logical thinking and realistic thinking and the pragmatic thinking and the economic thinking and the fair thinking, he is true. Japan is too big. World's second or third economy, and it cannot protect its own country? It's a mystery in the real meaning. So, he will say, "Protect yourself, or if Japan needs American protection or umbrella of nuclear weapon of the United States, Japan should pay more budget for defense cost of the U.S."

It will be choiceable for Japan. Of course, we can pay more or instead of that, we can protect by ourselves. It will give us a choice, but it does not mean Donald Trump is crazy or he's a tyrant. But he treated Japan as an equal partner and from the standpoint of equality and fairness, he said so. "Japan should protect herself. And South Korea, also, have enough power to protect itself from North Korea."

And especially, we must have keen attention on his opinion about the Spratly Islands issue. He said, "America should make more military force surge to the Spratly Islands." It indicates that he has the strategic idea or viewpoint he can rely on. He knows well.

Xi Jinping thinks that China is too big for America to have separation with, but it's not true. He has two kinds of thinking. One is the economic thinking, and another one is world justice. He's a businessman, so he can think about the real equal balance between China and America.

I think, in these 25 years, China has had huge economic growth, but Japan has been in status quo and America in trade deficit in these decades. It means America has been too weak in the economic trade meaning. So, he will change from the first point and this is good for creating world peace and world power balance, I think so.

7

AMERICA SHOULD PLAY THE ROLE OF WORLD POLICEMAN AGAIN

And if I predict the next year and the following years of the United States and the world, I think we can sleep well, or we will sleep well from next year, because Japan and the United States reliance can be the world's main engine again, and the fundamental value of the U.S. and Japan will continue as the global criteria, so we can co-prosper for the next eight years. So, the result of the American presidential race was good for Japan and the world. We must check the world balance.

And of course, Mr. Barack Obama insisted on how to protect the human rights. It will be realized by the stronger America again, I think so. The world can have several hegemonic countries, but the main value for the human rights must be one. It is the meaning of democracy, freedom, and how to make world prosperity, and check the tyranny of the evil country. America should cooperate with another country and should play the role of the world policeman again, I think so.

This is my idea on the next day of the election of the United States presidency.

Question 1

Guidance on how to unite the divided America after the election

Thank you very much, Master Okawa. Thank you for your deep insights and wisdom.

My question is on how to unite the people of America again because this election seems to have divided people into red or blue clearly. But in last night's Mr. Donald Trump's speech, he said, "It's time for us to come together as one united people." So, I would appreciate if you could give us guidance on how to create "united people."

Question by Kazuhiro Ichikawa
Senior Managing Director of Happy Science
Chief Director of International Headquarters

Answer 1

OK. As I told already, Mr. Trump is not a person who is comprehended by American mass media and Japanese mass media. He's quite a different person. He made too many extreme speeches, but in reality, he is a very moderate person and he has a very soft touch. He can keep very soft-touch relationship between people because he has lived to 70 years old and he has been a great businessman. So, he knows a lot about that. It's just been his strategy because he was not a politician. And he was not expected, so it was his strategy.

But as you heard yesterday, when he made a victory speech, firstly he said, "I received the call from Hillary Clinton, Mrs. Hillary Clinton, and she said, 'Congratulations.'" He appreciated her and he said she did a good job. This means he's quite different in reality. He knows, in real meaning, what it is, what she is, what he is, what man is, what men are, what the world is, what the economy is, and what politics is.

Hillary criticized him that he has no experience in politics and he has no experience of the army, and that he is the last man who can be believed to be a commander-in-chief, I mean the head of the American

Army, the world number one army, and can use the nuclear code for nuclear missiles. Hillary criticized like that. But it's a misunderstanding on him. He can be a great politician and he is the most suitable person for commander-in-chief.

Commander-in-chief means he is the leader of the army and is required almighty capacity for everything. It's not only for war strategy, but also the commander-in-chief must know the world economy, world relationship and the morality, how to deal with another people of another country. But he knows in reality.

And he insisted the separation of the intruders from foreign countries. Now, at this time, it is essential for the United States to rethink about that, but it's not the eternal policy. I think so.

And in reality, American economy has been in great recession in these several years. They were replaced by foreign immigrants and they experienced a lot of dumping from Asian and African countries, so this is a very essential point for the rebirth of the United States in the economic meaning. He says he will build the [*laughs*] Trump wall between Mexico and the USA. It's interesting. He declared clearly, so will he try to build Trump wall or not? It's very exciting.

But he will use this condition for negotiation between Mexico and the United States, I think so. It's very important for the United States, how to stop the intruders from Mexico, especially people who have tendency to be criminals and tendency to be drug addicts. So, it's very important. It's the cancer within the United States. So, someone should check and stop this tendency.

I don't think he will make a new long wall of the Trump wall, but instead of that, he will save the intruder population from Mexico and check them if they are the criminal tendency or not, or drug-related people or not. It is very important for America.

But he, himself, is German-oriented person and his wife is from the east part of Europe, so he knows a lot about the one aspect of the immigrant that is good for America: to provide new, excellent people from the world, because America is a country of dream. So, every people or the people who want to succeed or want to come to the United States, some of them are very excellent and can be America's new engine for the future. He knows about that.

But before that, he must recheck about the immigrant policy, I think so. People of the world are astonished by his presidency, but I don't think so. In the next one year, he will think considerably and will make new strategy about that.

So, the dividing country's problem will change in the next real change of the United States. It's Obama's declaration eight years ago that he said he will change America. But the country's tendency is not good for the American future. So, Donald Trump will make real change for the rebirth of the great America or greater America. It's OK, we can accept.

America has many deficits, as you know, of course, the gun control problem, drug problem, or the difference between the rich and the poor. Of course, they have a lot of problems, but this is one of the greatest dream country of the world, so America should shine more and more. It will lead the world into the future, I guess so. So, the problem they say, "the divided America," will be conquered by Trump's real personality and realistic capability of his new governance power, I think so.

Question 2

Will Trump's lower tax policy be successful?

Master Okawa, thank you very much for today's lecture. Your lecture is very encouraging. Thank you very much.

Let me ask about the economic policy, especially tax policy. Mr. Obama's tax policy is higher tax, making a big government and redistributing the income to the minority people, especially poor people. Then, the U.S. had the worst economic recovery. So, it didn't succeed. And now, Mr. Trump said drastic lower tax such as 15 percent corporate tax. Now, the U.S. corporate tax is over 35 percent. People think this is ridiculous, so nobody believed that kind of policy and the mass media ignored his policy.

However, Master Okawa, you insisted the same kind of lower tax policy when you founded the Happiness Realization Party. So, what do you think about this kind of drastic lower tax policy to adopt in the U.S. and maybe in Japan?

Question by Yuki Oikawa
Director of Foreign Affairs
Happiness Realization Party

∽ *Answer 2* ∽

OK. It's a very important point. But Donald Trump will realize lower tax policy, I think so. It's essential for the rebirth of the United States. I said 15 percent is enough for private companies. When you earn 100, if you were taken 15 from government or another lower bureaucracy, it's enough, I think so. Thirty-five percent is too much. No work, but gain the profit only. It's a bad government, I think so. It's not an effective government, I think so.

Effective government means lower tax and make the private sector prosper more and more. It's the fundamental guideline for them. For example, even in Japan, the Abe government insisted that the Japanese corporations have inner money, about 370 trillion yen or so. He is targeting to get this inner-saving money from companies and to let them consume like Edo era's people, just consume and it will make prosperity of the economy, but this is a bad policy. In accordance with Japanese tradition, it's a bad *Tono-sama* [lord] president. We must save for the crisis, the future turbulence of the company's great decision, government's mistake, or foreign pressure. We must save money for the future. It is essential.

But there are greater-government policy people who can dream that a greater government or a big government will lead to an equal society. They are dreaming like that. That just means the idea of the communist declaration, I think so. Japan already has been caught by this kind of lure and if Mr. Trump changes the tax policy within the United States, Japan cannot insist the same policy. Japan must change their mind.

Government should work especially for non-profit area, I mean the realm. Profitable realm, it's for privatized, I mean the usual common companies area. And the nation's economy will receive more prosperity. Greater government, if in real meaning greater, it's OK, but if greater means just the gigantic government, it means it hires people who cannot work in the private realm, that kind of non-capable people, and pay their income from tax and lower the lost-job population.

Government usually wants to move to hire the jobless people and pay them from tax, so it means the company or people who worked hard and saved cost and produced profit will be taken more tax. And this tax will be used for the people who don't have a job now.

In some meaning, it's a good sense to create jobs, but in another sense, bureaucrats or bureaucracy means the incapable people or people who don't have enough power to earn money or make their living. It's the meaning of bureaucrats. So, the expansion of the members of bureaucracy is a bad news for the country, especially for future economy.

In Japan, we pay 1.5 times the income for public servants. It's bigger than the private sector. For example, if you get 400,000 yen for your winter bonus, a Japanese public servant can get 600,000 yen for his or her bonus. Why? Japanese government cannot answer this question, "Why?" If they pay more than private companies, it will mean the raise of the economy and the growth of the economy. Mr. Abe thinks like that. But it's bad, I mean, it's not the management-style thinking.

So, Donald Trump will change the story. Hillary criticized that the "trumped-up and trickle down," it means the economic pyramid, when the top of the economic pyramid becomes more wealthy, it will trickle down to the lower part of the people.

But it's false, Hillary said so. And democratic people, the poor people, are likely to think to get money forcibly from the upper class and give the helicopter money to the lower side of the people. In some meaning, it sounds like Christian thinking. Like Jesus said, if you are rich, give all things to others, but in reality, a businessman cannot do so. If he is management class, he cannot do so because he has responsibility to pay money and make the company a going concern company. It will need profit for him to keep his company and to hire his followers, so it's quite different.

America is not a country of Catholics, America is a Protestant country originally, so Protestants agree to get profit for prosperity and its prosperity will trickle down to every person of the nation. It is the Protestant thinking, I think so. So, if one is clever and wiser, he can get more money. It's reasonable. But if he has enough consciousness for God or poor people, he will use his income for good things. It depends on him, but he can do it.

It is one of the American traditions. It's more than Japanese tradition. Japanese tradition is less than American tradition. American people can do that, like Bill Gates or so. They can make great money, but they can use this money for the poor people of the world. It is America's most beautiful mind. I think so. Don't forget about the beautiful tradition.

So, America should not be a communist country. Japan also, deny to be a communist country. It means to just stop the gigantic government. It means a not effective government. The first step for that is to lower the tax rate and let the private companies do more for a better world. It is the main concept, I think so.

Question 3

How will America's relation with Russia change?

Thank you very much for today's speech, and much congratulations for yesterday.

May I ask a little more about diplomacy, especially the relationship with Russia? Master, you were talking about the Syrian War and how Mr. Trump would cease the fire. Also, Mr. Putin says the same thing. The Syrian War is called a proxy war. So, how can they deal with this war, for example? In this sense, Russia is fatal for America to be the world's policeman. Would you talk especially about the relation with Russia?

Question by Kazuhiro Takegawa
Director General of International Public Relations Division, Happy Science

Answer 3

OK. World question is how the relationship between Russia and America will change next year. My answer is, it will be for a good direction.

Mr. Putin and Mr. Trump can understand each other, as reported from the mass media. The mass media cannot understand the real meaning. Even Ms. Hillary Clinton cannot understand.

Usually, American people, especially the Republican people, think of Russia as an enemy. So, in the enemy country of Russia, the dictatorship of Putin has been continuing and Mr. Putin praised Mr. Trump, "He's a good man, and a reliable man." Donald Trump also said Putin has greater leadership than, as you know, Mr. Obama.

He's an honest person, I think so. This means "hero knows hero" as an old saying says so. *Eiyuu, eiyuu wo shiru*, "hero knows hero," that's the reason. So, Donald Trump and Mr. Putin also can esteem another person's power, capability, or virtue. They know each other and can respect each other.

So, the relationship between the two countries will be better next year. And I predict, in the next year, I mean 2017, in one year, the problem of the IS will end because Russia and American relationship will determine the conclusion. Russia will have a power on Syria and America will regain the power on Iraq, and the IS will disappear in the end. That's the conclusion.

And during this process, we must make a good operation, how to reduce the killed people, I mean the non-army people, and how to save women and children. So, it will need American great will and Russian great will. The problem will end next year, I think so.

And the relationship between Putin and Trump will change the relationship between China and Japan, China and Russia, and China and North Korea. Mr. Xi Jinping thinks that Hillary will be stronger than Donald Trump, but in reality, it's quite contrary to that. Donald Trump will be stronger than Hillary because he knows the economy and foreign trade very deeply.

So, I can guess how he will deal with China. He must think from the standpoint of the world economic equality or balance, and soon he will realize China's expansion rate is quite extraordinary. What's the problem? It's a problem of foreign currency exchange rate and the problem of the import tax rate.

He, Donald Trump, will call back the American corporations from China to the United States, and Japan will follow in some meaning. Japanese corporations will withdraw their companies from China to Japan and to inner production.

It's very essential. America changed its economic style from the first, second, third grades to the fourth grade, it means more than the service realm, for example, the financial planning level or like that. It means it's just the leverage for the economic field, not the real economy.

But Donald Trump realizes that the real economy is essential for the fundamentals of the country. He will regain the industry of the United States again. But he forgot that Japan doesn't have import taxes for American cars. American cars don't sell in Japan because they are too big to run on the Japanese roads. They are too big, too expensive, and too strong for Japan.

I once bought an American car, a Lincoln, for one year. It was about three tons and I could not turn right or left on the road enough because Japanese roads are very narrow. So, we could not control the car.

I bought that car because before that, there occurred the Aum affairs* in Japan, and Aum people wanted to shoot me. So, I bought a Lincoln and it, of course, had protection for bullets. But it was too heavy and I could not open the door by myself [*laughs*] [*audience laugh*].

But the positive point is, if I ride on the Lincoln, when we crash with a dump car, we can survive, even at that time. When we crash with a usual Japanese car, they will fly away, [*laughs*] so it's a positive point. But I sold it within a year because it's not so easy for Japan to use that kind of heavy, deluxe car. And, how do I say, everyone could know who I am and what this car was, so it was not so good. So, I changed it to a Toyota car [*audience laugh*]. This is the reason. Donald Trump never thinks about that, but he will know soon.

* Aum Shinrikyo, a self-proclaimed new religion in Japan, committed an abduction and murder, and the subway sarin attack from Feb. to Mar. 1995. Happy Science had been criticizing Aum even before such events occurred and was cooperating with the police in investigating those cases. Later, the leader of Aum who was the mastermind behind the plan was given the death penalty.

Chapter 2

FREEDOM, JUSTICE, *and* HAPPINESS

Held October 2, 2016
Crowne Plaza Times Square Manhattan, New York

This lecture was held in New York
about a month before the presidential election.

Please love each other.

America should not be divided.

And the world also.

We must run through the earth of "Love."

We must live through the age of "Mercy."

The real trust will be built upon "Honesty."

And,

I dare say, now is the time to believe in God.

God has already saved America.

"He" has already forecasted a new age.

Go beyond "Hatred."

God has never indicated "Righteousness" of terrorism.

Let's cherish the dream of "World Peace" again.

Ryuho Okawa
Master and CEO of Happy Science Group
November 29, 2016

This preface was given for the publication of this lecture.

1

NEW YORK IS A LITTLE DIFFERENT FROM EIGHT YEARS AGO

Hello, everyone. Hello. Hello. I came back. Thank you for coming today.

Today's theme is very difficult, "Freedom, Justice, and Happiness." This is fit for the presidential election theme. I think so. I just want to say in terms of religion. I'm not Donald Trump and I'm not Hillary Clinton; I'm just Ryuho Okawa. But I'm not a Japanese. I'm a universal man, so I'll say in terms of the universal stage.

So, let's begin. I have only 30 minutes to make a speech for you. I usually speak a lot, more than one hour or one hour and a half, so it's very difficult for me to shorten my speech. I cannot speak on idle things, so I'll say just my feeling I had when I came here again.

To tell the truth, NY is a little different, I think so. It's very, in some meaning, silent, in some meaning, no vitality, and in some meaning, no philosophy. I found that. I just found that a coffee shop, Starbucks, is spreading, just like Japan. It's remarkable, I think. Eight years ago, I came here, but I couldn't see such kind of Starbucks, so it's one point.

What does this fact mean for the American economy? I again watched *The Devil Wears Prada* on TV, it was a movie of 2006 before the great depression. At that time, the beautiful devil requested her secretary to order the Starbuck coffee, only Starbucks coffee.

But even in Japan, directors of great companies don't want to buy Starbucks coffee because it's for the common people. They hesitate to buy Starbucks, though it's expensive, maybe three times as much as usual coffee in Japan. But I drink 30-dollar coffee or 15-dollar coffee, you know? A little different [*laughs*].

So, my impression is that America has changed a little. Upper level of American people is fewer and fewer. And the bottom people in economic meaning and political meaning are also becoming fewer and fewer, and the middle class is becoming larger and larger. It's just my impression.

2

AMERICA HAS THE MISSION TO MAKE A NEW DREAM FOR THE WORLD

But in these eight years, it's been an Obama presidency. I sometimes say in Japan that Obama's aim is Japanization* in the U.S.A. I felt like that because he hates the suit-wearing people in Manhattan, especially in Wall Street, like me in my early years. He hates such kind of people and, of course, he set free the African-American people. It's a good thing, I think so, but he hates wealthy, capable people.

And now, Hillary Clinton, she's of course a nice, smart, and clever woman. I respect her a lot. But she just looks at the middle layer, the middle-class people. How to widen the middle class, that is her policy, I think so.

And in the latest debate, she said, "Trumped up,

*The author has repeatedly pointed out that Obama was headed toward Japanization, or toward making America become like Japan. Since the beginning of 2009, soon after the Obama administration took power, the author has been saying that Obama's goals, which are to establish a medical insurance program, to narrow economic disparity through distributing income, to reduce discrimination by creating a homogeneous society, and a conciliatory foreign policy, have already come true in Japan.

trickle down*. Trumped up, trickle down, Trumped up, trickle down." Three times. But that is not good, I think. She lacks some kind of economic sense. "Trumped up" are very interesting words. But one of the American problems is that you have the tendency of hating or have envy for wealthy people.

In the inner case, it will do a good thing for security and protect the occurrence of criminalities. But from the standpoint of the world, if America, the United States of America, hesitates to let people be wealthy, it will be the end of America. We think so. We means people except Americans. It's an American dream, one of the American dreams.

So, America is not for Americans only. It's for the leaders of the world. I think so. You have the mission to make a new dream for the world. A new mission to show the future picture of the world. But this is just missing, I felt, in New York.

* Trickle-down (effect) is an economic idea that says the wealth gained by the rich people will trickle down to the lower-income, poor people.

3

BE THE "UNITED STATES OF AMERICA," NOT THE "DIVIDED STATES OF AMERICA"

I stayed in America, at first, in the early stage of Mr. Ronald Reagan's presidency. It's the early 1980's. I worked on Wall Street at the time.

And next, I came here in 1996 during the presidency of Bill Clinton. At that time, the Japanese dream had been destroyed by Clinton diplomacy*, especially in terms of economy. He used the words, "global standard," and it destroyed the Japanese banking system. So, we suffered for 25 years in this depression. After that, I came here in 2006 during the presidency of Bush Jr.

And after that, in 2008. The last time I gave my lecture. It was before the appearance of Barack Obama,

* During Bill Clinton's presidency from 1993-2000, America traded less with Japan and more with China. This was called, "Japan-passing." It helped expand China's economy and suppressed Japan's economy. In addition, when the BIS Regulations were forced on Japan during his term, Japanese financial institutions took back their loans from businesses, leading to many business bankruptcies. Thus, a lot of Japan's economic competitiveness was lost.

his presidency. So, at the time, the great depression of America just started, as the former Fed Chairman, Mr. Greenspan, and the prime minister of Japan at the time, Mr. Aso, said. They said that is the disaster of once in one hundred years.

But after I gave a lecture here in New York in 2008 on September 28, I returned to Japan and gave a lecture on October 5. "This is not a great depression, you don't anticipate about that. This is not a great depression." I said so. After that, Mr. Aso, at that time the Japanese prime minister, and Mr. Greenspan said that it's a great disaster, but my prediction held true at that time.

And now, I feel that I must insist a new style or new vision of the United States. You must not love the "Divided States of America." You must be the "United States of America." "Divided States" is not good for everyone of the world. Be concerned about this truth.

We can watch on TV through, for example, CNN or like that, the battle between two candidates. They are apt to assault one another, speak ill of the other person. But we, Japanese, don't like such kind of tendency. Please stress on their own opinion, policy, or characteristic idea, I think so.

So, this country should not be the "Divided United

States." Be "America, the United States." Red states and blue states should aim, at the end, to the same goal. America must be the protector of the world, I think. This is your mission.

But from their speech, I found some kind of isolationism. It's just a game, but in the true meaning, if they insist from their heart of their own, it's a problem, I think so.

4

THE GROWING CRISIS OF ASIA

During the Obama presidency, Mr. Obama got the Nobel Peace Prize. It's good for him, but it's bad for the world, especially for Japan, especially for Asian countries. He loves the Nobel Prize. But when someone gets the Noble Prize, after that, there comes tragedy, in history. It's a tendency of the Nobel Prize history.

During these eight years, the crisis of Asia has become greater and greater. We are now, "we" means in this context Japanese people, surrounded by the countries which have nuclear weapons. So, now we must decide how to deal with these countries. How can we punish them?

It's difficult. We don't fight against enemies. It's forbidden by our constitution. And America has great deficit in their budget. So, they want to ask the Japanese, "Give more money, or protect yourselves," I think. Mr. Donald Trump said Japan is too big to protect. He said so. It's true. I think he is an honest man. He is honest. Japan is too big.

But it is very difficult to make the decision or to change the direction of Japan, or the form of Constitution of Japan, including the emperor system. So, we don't have enough time. The North Korean problem alone is too much for Japanese people.

How should we deal with that North Korean problem? If it were not for Obama's presidency, and if Bush Jr. were the president these eight years, he must have given more strong words to North Korea and could have stopped their military expansion.

5

A NEW PHILOSOPHY FROM THE U.S.A. TO THE WORLD

A more difficult problem is China's problem. China is expanding, and wants to have the new great hegemony of the China Empire. I love China, of course; we have been friends these 2,000 years. We learned a lot from them and our economic intercourse is very deep and high. But here, I want to say that they lack philosophy.

But in some meaning, they have a small philosophy. It's pragmatism*. You, American people, have already known pragmatism since more than 100 years ago. You obeyed this kind of pragmatism philosophy in the practical meaning. Its criteria is just "useful or not," "available or not," or "profitable or not." This is the character of pragmatism. Now, China has no philosophy, but if they have a philosophy, it is pragmatism. So, both America and China have the philosophy of pragmatism.

So now, I insist that you transform into another

* A practical philosophy that originated in America. It became well-known through *Pragmatism* by William James in 1910. The central idea is, "whether or not a concept or proposal is true depends on its practicality."

country. You should have a new philosophy from now on. You earned a lot, of course, and you became rich, of course, but after that, "pragmatism only" is very miserable for humankind because we are made from God. God's desire is greater than pragmatism.

This is very important. Your future is "how to sophisticate your philosophy." In another meaning, you have many kinds of Christian groups or Christian thinking, but you need to make a new type of innovation from the old type of Christian tendency, philosophy, or thinking.

We just feel from the movies of Hollywood that you are seeking for a new hero, and the new hero replaces the god of America, I think so. But hero is hero. You must need more than a hero. America is a great country, so you need a new god of America. It means the philosophy which can save the world. It's beyond pragmatism, beyond capitalism.

China also became a capitalist country in the economic meaning, but they don't have enough political democracy. I think democracy is very difficult for more-than-one-billion-population country. They want to be controlled by tyrannic leadership, but they may be suffering from this truth. And they cannot decide by voting, so they need a new type of thinking. This new type of thinking must be dispatched from the U.S.A.

6

LEADERS OF THE WORLD NEED GOD'S VIEW

So, you must think another thing. The citizens of the United States are not Americans. You are world citizens, the world leaders. You must decide your freedom, justice, and happiness in terms of the Earth. Don't think about your country only. You are the leaders of the world. Don't disregard this point.

I also want to say to Ms. Hillary Clinton and Mr. Donald Trump. They are good woman and man, but they need this viewpoint. They need God's view because they are the leaders of the new America.

To tell the truth, these eight years of American declining period means the dangerous period of the world. It's in East Asia, West Asia, Europe, Africa, and Russia. There are a lot of new hegemonic countries in the world, but no one can persuade them. The UN doesn't work now.

So, the only power is the U.S. The U.S. must be strong, stronger, strongest. It's your mission. Be brave and have mission in your heart. Your academic work, your economic work, your political work, and your diplomatic work, your mission, it's not for America only.

Please go beyond America and see from the standpoint of the Earth. Earthly happiness, it's very important.

7

AMERICA, BE GREATER

We, Japanese people, are trying to change now because in Japan, there is the new God, as you know. So, it's changing now, but we need a little more time to change. We must decide how to live, how to be a leader, and how to be friends for all the people of the world.

So, America and Japan, the two countries, must be great leaders of the world from this year, for at least three hundred years, I hope so.

You need a new philosophy for that.
It's the definition of God.
It's the real meaning of God.
Believing in God is good.
But what's the meaning of God's will?
This is the starting point of a new philosophy.
This is your mission.
This is what I want to say today.
Be great, greater.
With great power comes great responsibility.
You, American people, have great responsibility for the world.
Please keep this truth in your mind.

That is the conclusion of the lecture.

Question 1

There is a decline in religion in America. There is an apathy and skepticism about it. And Americans are very headstrong. How do you go about convincing Americans that religion is right and now is the time?

Answer 1

Conquer 9.11 and the great depression

OK, America has been changing from September 11 and the new great depression. These two events changed America completely, radically, I think so. But please conquer these two facts.

After September 11, America attacked the country of Iraq and after that, there have been a lot of problems. One is terrorism, and another one is a different kind of reflection about, "Are we right to kill the people of Asia?" That is the American instability.

And after 2008, you experienced, "American economy is the right one or not?" "The people who are working to make money at Wall Street, are they good people? Is their dealing process or method good or not, is it false or not?" So, you cannot have confidence in your way of prosperity.

But now, I'll tell you. Sometimes people make mistakes. Everyone has chances to make a mistake, but everyone also has chances to rebuild himself, to rebuild his company, to rebuild his country, and to rebuild the world. So, don't look back on the past too much. Please change your mind toward the brighter future.

Mr. Obama, when he appeared, insisted "change is important." You expected from him, but his change is a little different, I think. America should be greater and could show the greater future of the world. You must make dreams for the people of the world.

Don't hesitate to protect the peaceful people from terrorism. And don't be afraid of terrorism too much. Your fear is the problem, I think. Freedom from terrorism is very important. America is shrinking now because of the fear of terrorism.

But terrorism is terrorism. Terrorism is lower than militarism. America is the greatest country of God's military. So, never think too much about terrorism.

Japanese people don't think about terrorism because we don't kill each other and foreign people don't kill us. But we don't have enough power to save the world. Only America has the power.

America receives the glory of God

China is a greater country now, but they need something else. I mean, this is not democracy only; this is the freedom from Hell. They are suppressed by dictatorship. In some meaning, in a short period it's acceptable. But now, more than 50 years have passed since then, so now is the time to change China. Now is the time to change Russia. Now is the time to change the Philippines and Vietnam. And now is the time to say, "Japan, you are too big to protect. Japan should stand up."

So, please be confident of yourself. America is great. America is strong. America receives the glory of God! We are now still shedding light upon you. You are the leaders. You are the world destiny!

So, be brave, be strong, and have responsibility for all the world. Please say it to Donald Trump and Hillary Clinton. You are not alone. You are the leaders. You must receive God's command. You are the modern prophets.

Don't think about small things too much. Be brave and be pure in mind. It comes from real love. The definition of love is very easy. Just as Jesus Christ said, "Believe in God and believe your neighbors." That's the checkpoint of "true love or not."

So, from love to justice. From love to freedom. From love to happiness. This is the republic of love. And this is the democratic country based on God's love.

Believe in a miracle of today

Don't use or depend too much on scientific technology only. American people use more than seven hours watching television*, but please abandon this bad habit and read my books [*audience laugh*]. This will open the new age. Please tell them about that. Read good books. I have already written more than 2,100 books. It's beyond human capacity. This is a miracle, also. Please believe in this miracle. This is just the reality. Don't believe in it, just check it. No one can do such kind of things except Gautama Buddha of India. He taught a lot for 45 years. All of his teachings became testament. This is a great deed.

Now, I gave lecture more than 2,500 times, and my

* According to a 2016 study, Americans spend an average of about 5 hours watching television. Adding time spent on the web via computers and smartphones would increase this number to over 7 hours.

books are more than 2,100 titles. Can you understand? My teachings are all transferred into books. This is a miracle of today. This is just the proof of Buddha, Savior, or the Second Coming, you know?

Question 2

You are always giving us light, love and power. Today is like a miracle for all of us, having you here. I have one question. Nowadays, many people don't truly know what justice is. Although it isn't finalized yet, what would you like to say to the next president the most? What would you like for him or her to do the most?

Answer 2

The next president must be tough

Ah, I already researched; half of you are supporting Democrats, and half of you are supporting Republicans, so it's a difficult "divided party hall." It's a little difficult.

But I think, during Bill Clinton's presidency, we suffered a lot. And at that time, China became a gigantic country and a hegemonic country, so we suffered a lot from Mr. and Mrs. Clinton already. Never again, I hope, indeed. But it's a secret [*audience laugh and applause*].

Of course, Hillary Clinton is smart and she can break the glass ceiling. It's true. And if she becomes the next president, this next American politics will be very effective for working ladies. But the next president must cooperate with and compete with China's Xi Jinping and Russia's Vladimir Putin. Then, the next president must be tough, I mean.

Trump will make America a greater country

Donald Trump is not so nice nowadays, but when he was 42 years old, he was very smart and a beautiful, nice looking guy, and clever. When he was 40 or 50, he was very good. But he is 70. I have 10 more years until his age, so I'm also worried about his health. But he has stamina as he says.

I spiritually researched his past life in Japan, and at that time, he declared that he was the first president of the United States, George Washington. He said so. It means he will rebuild this America again.

I want to believe in his words, he will remake and rebuild this country. You might feel like he is rude, or he speaks ill of others too much. But it's not his real figure. He's an honest man. He's a reliable man. I prefer Donald Trump. He will make America a greater country, I think so.

If you fail to choose Donald Trump, you will continue declining because Mrs. Clinton is no more than Mr. Obama. That's the conclusion. It means an Asian crisis, it means a Western Asian crisis, and it means a Russian crisis. And of course, the next great problem is China empire's hegemony.

So, America, be great. I ask America to be great. It means Mr. Trump is suitable. But this is my political opinion, not the religious opinion.

Jesus may like Hillary Clinton, I know. But in the political context, I think that you should choose Mr. Donald Trump because he has the might to solve the world's problems. He will change America. He is an honest man. He is a reliable man. He will rebuild a new America. I hope so.

So, in this point, the opinion is different between Jesus Christ and I. But I am the "Father" of Jesus Christ [*audience laugh*], so please rely on me. It's your success, I think so.

PART II

Chapter 3

SPIRITUAL INTERVIEW *with* GEORGE WASHINGTON

Revealing Donald Trump's Hidden Identity

Held September 22, 2016
Special Lecture Hall, Happy Science, Tokyo

Today, American people are apt to think too small.

Please remember the good old days and think about

America's Founding Father, "George Washington."

Now is the day to rebuild the United States.

"Think Big" and restart the movement toward

"Greater America."

This book is the true Spiritual Interview with George Washington.

You'd easily find the fountain of new wisdom.

This is the voice of God in disguise.

Please believe your new hope and future.

Master Ryuho Okawa
October 11, 2016

From the Preface given for the book, America Gasshukoku Kenkoku no Chichi George Washington no Reigen [*The Founding Father of the United States - Spiritual Interview with George Washington*] (*Tokyo: IRH Press, 2016*).

George Washington (1732 - 1799)

An American military official and politician. He was born as a child of a plantation owner and he, himself, gained great wealth through managing the plantation. He grew to fame as the commander of the British colony military fighting for the French in the French and Indian War in 1775. After the Battles of Lexington and Concord in 1775, he was appointed as commander-in-chief by the Continental Army and fought for American independence. After his resignation from commander-in-chief, he was elected as the president of the constitutional convention. Through the first American presidential election in 1789, he was elected as the first president and laid the foundation of the federal system. He came to be called America's "founding father," his portrait is now printed on the dollar bill, and his name is now used for the capital, an aircraft carrier, and a university.

Interviewers from Happy Science*:

Masayuki Isono

Executive Director
Chief of Overseas Missionary Work Promotion Office
Deputy Chief Secretary
First Secretarial Division Religious Affairs Headquarters

Yuta Okawa

Managing Director, Deputy Chief of CEO's Office
Religious Affairs Headquarters
Advisor of General Headquarters
Activity Promotion Strategist of Political Headquarters,
Activity Promotion Strategist of International Headquarters

Shugaku Tsuiki

Executive Director
Principal of Happy Science Institute of Government and Management

This chapter is the transcript of spiritual messages given in English by the spirit of George Washington. These spiritual messages were channeled through Ryuho Okawa by his extraordinary spiritual power. The opinions of the spirits do not necessarily reflect those of Happy Science Group. For the mechanism behind spiritual messages, see end section.

---

* Interviewers are listed in the order that they appear in the transcript. Their professional titles represent their positions at the time of the interview.

1

AMERICA'S FOUNDING FATHER WASHINGTON APPEARS

MASAYUKI ISONO

Now, we will start the spiritual interview with George Washington. Thank you very much, Master Ryuho Okawa.

RYUHO OKAWA

OK. Then, let's start. We are going to New York soon*, so the spiritual teaching of George Washington is very important, I think. This is the starting point of the United States of America and today, we have an opportunity to hear from him. So, we'd like to try. Then, is it OK?

We'd like to summon the spirit of the first president of the United States, George Washington. Mr. George Washington, the spirit of George Washington, would you come down here? We'd like to summon the spirit of George Washington, the first president of the United States.

* On October 2nd, 2016, Master Okawa gave an English lecture titled, "Freedom, Justice, and Happiness" at Crowne Plaza Times Square in Manhattan, New York.

ISONO
Good morning.

GEORGE WASHINGTON
Hmm...

ISONO
Are you...

WASHINGTON
Good morning.

ISONO
...President George Washington?

WASHINGTON
Yeah.

ISONO
Thank you very much for coming here today. It's a great honor to have you here. We will be more than happy to ask you several questions about yourself, the mission of America and its current situation. Is it OK?

WASHINGTON
OK, OK, OK.

ISONO
OK. Thank you very much. Firstly, I'd like to ask you about the mission of the United States because you are the founding president of the United States. The United States has been a great nation, a leading nation of the world for the past several decades. So, could you tell us what the mission of the United States of America is?

WASHINGTON
Ahh...the United States is the new utopia of the world that was founded in the past 200 years. I had a special mission from God. "George Washington, please open a new world. This is the Land of Canaan* for you with the new immigrants from Europe. This nation will be the new leader of the world after the 18th or 19th century." So, this was a great mission. God told me, "You are the new Adam, the new Moses," or something like that. This was my mission.

America is the greatest country in the world now. At

* The land that God promised to give to the Israelites in the Old Testament. In the bible, it is described as "land flowing with milk and honey." Moses led the Israelites out of Egypt and headed to the Land of Canaan.

the time of my presidency, it was a small country. The country's land was very huge but the country's power itself was very, very small. We became independent from the United Kingdom by the help of France. So at first, we were people who ran away from the United Kingdom and other countries, but nowadays, we are the champions of the world.

ISONO
OK.

2

IN THE AMERICAN PRESIDENTIAL ELECTION, HE SUPPORTS THE "HONEST MAN"

YUTA OKAWA
Thank you very much for coming to Happy Science today.

WASHINGTON
Uh-huh.

YUTA OKAWA

My first question is simple. What is your hot issue now?

WASHINGTON

Hot issue?

YUTA OKAWA

Yes, in Heaven.

WASHINGTON

Heaven!?

YUTA OKAWA

Or from your viewpoint.

WASHINGTON

Or Hell? [*Laughs.*]

YUTA OKAWA

[*Laughs.*] I don't know. So…

WASHINGTON

[*Laughs.*] I'm joking. Hot issue is, of course, the American presidency.

YUTA OKAWA
Uh-huh.

WASHINGTON
The race for the presidency. Hot issue is how to knock down Hillary Clinton, of course [*laughs*].

YUTA OKAWA
[*Laughs.*] OK. So, I guess you're now supporting a candidate in the United States presidential election.

WASHINGTON
Uh-huh.

YUTA OKAWA
What's his name?

WASHINGTON
His name? It's the name for a *card* [*laughs*].

[*Interviewers laugh.*]

YUTA OKAWA
OK.

ISONO
Maybe a trump card?

WASHINGTON
Yeah, a *trump* card [*laughs*].

YUTA OKAWA
OK.

WASHINGTON
The American joker, you know?

ISONO
[*Laughs.*] Yes.

YUTA OKAWA
OK. I think the typical image of the first president, George Washington, was that he was very…

WASHINGTON
Honest!

YUTA OKAWA
Honest, yeah.

WASHINGTON
Reliable.

YUTA OKAWA
Reliable.

WASHINGTON
Responsible.

YUTA OKAWA
But the American people depict you as a very serious and calm person. That's our image about you. But…

WASHINGTON
Strong and what?

YUTA OKAWA
Strong, calm and…

WASHINGTON
Cor?

YUTA OKAWA
Calm.

WASHINGTON
Cold?

YUTA OKAWA
Calm.

WASHINGTON
Colb?

YUTA OKAWA
Very quiet, you know? Your image…

WASHINGTON
Ah, I know.

YUTA OKAWA
…in the movies, for example.

WASHINGTON
Image? Ah…

YUTA OKAWA
Yeah, the typical image of you. But now, the real Mr. Donald Trump is a little different…

WASHINGTON
OK, OK, OK, OK, OK.

YUTA OKAWA
...from your typical image, so...

WASHINGTON
I got it.

YUTA OKAWA
We may misunderstand your personality.

WASHINGTON
George Washington, the first president, was good at fighting, as you know. He was the commander-in-chief of the United States who fought against the United Kingdom. I am good at fighting.

Nowadays, we don't fight against our rivals with a sword, gun, arrow or something like that. We fight against our competitors using only words, so words are the weapon nowadays. This is the reason I changed my strategy. That's the reason. We, who want to be a statesman like a president or a governor, must fight against our rivals and huge mass media using words, so words are very important these days. That is our new weapon.

YUTA OKAWA
Thank you. Yeah, we agree with that opinion. Mr. Donald Trump, himself, is very honest, too.

WASHINGTON
Honest! Yeah, it's a good word. Please print these words in Gothic and in big print. "**Honest man. Honest man, Donald Trump!**" Oh, yeah, it's good.

YUTA OKAWA
Other existing politicians in Washington D.C. use superficial words, but they are hiding something, I feel. So, Mr. Donald Trump is very...

WASHINGTON
Honest! Yeah.

YUTA OKAWA
Yeah, honest.

WASHINGTON
Yeah, honest! Hmm.

YUTA OKAWA
It's his personality, I think.

WASHINGTON
It means I'm strong. Because of my strength, I can be honest. If politicians speak honestly, the mass media will attack them because of those words, so they want to hide their real thoughts. They use other words or hide their real political intentions.

So, these days, to be honest means to be strong. We are running through a field where bullets of mass media are flying from both sides, so it's very difficult. But I'm Captain America, so I can fight against them. My strength is my honesty.

YUTA OKAWA
Thank you very much.

3

ON RACIAL PROBLEMS IN CURRENT AMERICA

WASHINGTON
[*Sees Tsuiki attempting to ask a question.*] Ah, a silent man.

SHUGAKU TSUIKI
Ah, thank you very much.

WASHINGTON
He will speak nothing.

TSUIKI
Uh…

WASHINGTON
[*Laughs.*]

TSUIKI
Sorry, what I would like to ask you is about the ethnic problems. Now in the United States, one of the hot issues is the racial problem.

WASHINGTON
Racial problem. OK.

TSUIKI
One of the problems is the black people.

WASHINGTON
Black people.

TSUIKI
They are often shot by policemen*, and people get angry. What do you think about that?

WASHINGTON
Uh-huh. OK, we have a lot of racial problems. One is, of course, the black problem. Another is the Hispanic problem and yet another is, of course, the Islamic problem. We have at least these three problems.

So firstly, there is the black problem, but we already have a black president. I forgot his name. Was it Black Obama or something like that?

* On September 20th, 2016, a black man was shot to death with a gun by a white police officer in Charlotte, North Carolina. This incident is controversial because there is a possibility that the man was not armed. Similar cases have occurred in recent years, causing widespread protests in America.

ISONO

Yes, Obama.

WASHINGTON

Ah, is that his name? We have a black president, President "Black Obama." So, it's a good news for black people that a black person became the president. At the least, they can be a president in the future, the next president or in the 21st or 22nd century. This means that they have political power nowadays, so it's good.

The next issue might be the presidency for ladies. This is a chance for ladies to become a president. It means Hillary Clinton. However, I don't think she is a real lady [*laughs*]. She was the First Lady to Bill Clinton, so it's not the problem of sexual discrimination.

If another lady who has made her way up by herself became a candidate for the presidency, I will appreciate it. But Hillary Clinton's capability is a little different. She benefits from Bill Clinton's halo, her husband. So we, the American people, dislike two presidents coming from one couple. I think it's against democracy. That's not democracy. That belongs to personal benefits. So, this is another problem. OK. Then, the next is, ah, did you only ask me about the black problem?

TSUIKI
Ah, the black people, the Hispanic people and so on.

WASHINGTON
I don't dislike Hispanic people. But in reality, please analyze the social situation of the United States. We have a lot of crimes in our country and the reason why is the immigrants from Mexico. They come with drugs, the tendency of criminality and of course, mafia-like business style.

So, I don't hate them but I just ask them before they become real Americans, "Please love America, the United States of America." It's the fundamental condition for them to be American. If they want to destroy our country, I will and we will resist against their tendencies.

Mexican people have envy toward the wealthy people in the United States. So, they want to intrude into the United States and become rich. To be rich is not a good thing in itself. We want to be rich for the purpose of a good aim, I mean to help other people, to help build God's state in this world or to help other countries who suffer from intrusions from a huge country. Something like that. So, I want them to have a frame of mind as a true American. This is the problem.

Some of the Mexican people are good people, of course, but others just seek to get money. That's a problem. They want to get money and it's easy to grow rich using drugs and things like that. But in the end, it will mean the ruin of a healthy society, so I hate them in this meaning. Of course, I know equality and I respect equality of the people as the members of the United States, but we must love our country. That's the reason. And oh…another one?

YUTA OKAWA
Islamic…

WASHINGTON
Islamic, ah, it's difficult. It's a very difficult problem. Just now, we experienced an Islamic attack in New York*. It's troublesome for you too, because you are scheduled to hold a great lecture in New York. It's troublesome. He, meaning the criminal, is an American citizen, but he is an Islamic believer; he experienced being in a lot of Islamic countries and strengthened his faith. He did bad things against the U.S. citizens. If he wants to do so, he

* On September 17th, 2016, blasts in the roads of Chelsea, New York left 29 injured. An American man from Afghanistan was placed in custody as a suspect.

must go back to IS, Afghanistan or another country. He should not be an American citizen. That's what I think.

4

HE HELPED GOD MAKE A NEW CIVILIZATION

YUTA OKAWA

Historically, it was recorded that you hated Native Americans.

WASHINGTON

Hahaha.

YUTA OKAWA

Your words remain, "They, American Indians, are beasts of prey." However, it was also recorded that you were very kind to your own black slaves in your home. So, I think Mr. Trump's tendency is very similar to your opinion on racial problems. What was your thought on races?

WASHINGTON

Of course, this land of North America historically belonged to the Native Americans. But this land is very huge and affluent. It was a new Canaan, flowing with milk and honey. It was a new land of hope. We thought God would be pleased by the prosperity brought through advanced people. So, we came from Europe as the Pilgrim Fathers or in another name, Puritans.

We aimed at setting up a new country of God in this area. So, this was a heavenly battle between the god of Native American Indians and the god of Pilgrim Fathers. European gods wanted to be separated from their old-fashioned worship and wanted to set up a new religion and a new social movement, which in the political meaning, was an experiment of democratic politics in this world.

Of course, the Native American Indians had their properties and rights, but God hoped that we would become the new masters. So, we did our best. Our mission was to open the frontier for the future, a new frontier.

We succeeded in our plans. We got rich and we showed our gods the prosperity of the New America. In another name, this was called the New Atlantis. Therefore, this is a matter of civilization. If the original God wants to make a new civilization, it's good to help Him. That's the reason.

Yes, I hired 40 or at most, almost 100 black slaves. But at that time, this was allowed. So I, myself, was a successful planter and became a rich man. It's my typical feature to be a rich man. I was rich and also a good commander-in-chief who was good at fighting against enemies.

And in addition to that, I was a statesman or politician—in a good meaning. I can be called the first politician of the United States. It meant I could separate enemies from our friends, and after that, settle the problem between them. Also, I could settle the problem between dominant people and people who were under their control. This is the starting point of a politician or statesman. So, I had three functions: commander-in-chief, a rich planter and politician. This was a blessing for the new America. Haha!

ISONO
Thank you.

5

ON AMERICA'S FOREIGN POLICIES ON THE MIDDLE EAST AND RUSSIA

TSUIKI
I would like to ask a question about diplomacy.

WASHINGTON
Diplomacy? OK.

TSUIKI
How do you think the United States should cope with the Islamic State?

WASHINGTON
Hmm, ah, it's a little complicated. Firstly, I will support the country of Israel. They already have 200 nuclear missiles as former Secretary of State Powell spilled the beans*. On the other hand, Islamic countries don't have nuclear weapons nowadays. So, although there is a great

* On September 16th, 2016, it was reported that Colin Powell, a former secretary of state, sent a private email to an acquaintance mentioning that Israel held 200 nuclear weapons in March of 2015. In fact, Israel is considered to be a state with nuclear weapons, but has not formally admitted it.

difference between the population of Islamic countries and that of Israel, this power of nuclear bomb brings a balance of power. Therefore, we will support Israeli nuclear armament and we want to suppress the Islamic states. This is the first point.

Another point is Vladimir Putin. He has some kind of ambition to get Syria and control other Islamic states. We must cooperate with Mr. Putin. You must talk with him to make sure that the oil problem doesn't cause the next great war. Russia is in an economic crisis now, so they need new customers for their market. I must rebalance the power between Russia and America.

You already know that I love the isolation of America, but this is a misunderstanding. I don't just say isolation, I want to make new power in the United States *and* rebalance the world. After that, I want the United States to be the dominant country again and take new leadership. I will realize these desires in the next eight years.

6

ON AMERICAN AND WORLD ECONOMIES

YUTA OKAWA
Thank you. Next, I'd like to ask about the American and world economies.

WASHINGTON
OK.

YUTA OKAWA
President George Washington, your first career was a land surveyor. You made your living by that and you got rich. Now, Mr. Donald Trump is also very rich through trading real estates. His and your vocations are very similar, I guess.

WASHINGTON
Yeah.

YUTA OKAWA
I think you are one of the specialists on economy. So,

how can you revive the American economy and its position in the world economy?

WASHINGTON

Hmm...OK, OK. In my days, America was a small country in its activities and its power, in the economic meaning, of course. Now, it's number one in the world, although, it's declining a little.

The first problem is how to compete with the Chinese economy. Next one will be Japan, India or Germany. So, firstly, I'm thinking about the Chinese economy. They are doing too much. I don't want to say anything if they are acting within their own ability or capability, or within their real economic power. That's OK. But they have too much ambition. They want to become a hegemonic country and control the Asian and African countries in the political and economic meanings. They are even tempted to control the European countries. This is the great problem.

In addition to that, they have, for example, the South Asian islands problem, the Spratly Islands problem. The real problem is that they are approaching Russia; both China and Russia are cooperating in conducting joint exercises. They are cooperating to go against the United States.

So, I want to divide the two powers, China and Russia. I now want to make a new friendship with Vladimir Putin. Mr. Putin and I can be friends, I think, because he has great leadership. He is more skilled in controlling his political power than Mr. Obama. So, if I can become the next president—ah, not *can become*, I *will be* the next president—we, Putin and Donald Trump, or George Washington, will be good friends because we have respect for each other. We can estimate the political power or the capability of each other. So, we will cooperate with Russia.

Mr. Obama made a lot of mistakes. One of them is that he wanted to be an enemy of Russia because of the Crimean problem. I think Russia has the necessity to protect Crimean people because 65% of the Crimean people come from Russia. It's their duty. The EU also made a mistake. Thus, I support this point that Putin is not bad.

Another great mistake of Obama is that he is weak in the mind, so he wanted to decrease the power of nuclear weapons and tried to declare that the United States will never use nuclear weapons in its first attack. Now, the situation is unsettled because of the critiques from his colleagues. And South Korea and Japan are very afraid of North Korea, of course, so he must reconsider that.

I have the idea of controlling our war budget, but it doesn't mean that I want to destroy and weaken the American political power and the power of the U.S. army. I want to take a constructive way. I only want to focus on the effective matter. Before that, I or we need a conclusion, a decision against the new problem between two or three countries. I can make decisions, so it will be economical in the real meaning. I can use weapons in the context of the word, *economize*. This is not the weakness of the United States. This is efficient in managing our troops. We will, of course, ask our fellow countries, "If you want our cooperation, you have to pay your fair share." We will ask them. It's to strengthen America again.

7

ON PROBLEMS WITH NORTH KOREA

ISONO

OK. Thank you. I'd like to ask your thoughts on North Korean problems.

WASHINGTON

North Korean problems, OK.

ISONO

This year, North Korea has conducted several missile launch tests and nuclear tests.

WASHINGTON

Uh-huh.

ISONO

Now, the United Nations General Assembly is being held and the leaders of the world are discussing this issue. But I don't think they have a clear solution to this problem. So, I'd like to ask your thoughts on it.

WASHINGTON

Ah, OK, OK, OK. The North Korean problem itself is not so difficult. It's a small country. We can defeat them within one month, so it's not so difficult.

The difficult problem is China. China is supporting North Korea, in reality. So, we must ask them, "Which do you like better? North Korea or the free trade with Western countries?" We will or I will insist about this issue. I want to separate the combination between these two countries.

China wants to use North Korea as a tool or the right hand or left hand of the Chinese army when a new war occurs between them and the United States, Japan or South Korea. That's the reason China or Beijing spoke that it's not good to set the THAAD missiles* in the bases of South Korea because these can protect against the missiles of China. This means they are thinking about the North Korean army as their tools to protect China from other countries. So firstly, I must separate these two countries in the political context.

Next is how to separate the combination between

* Terminal High Altitude Area Defense missile. An interception system to shoot down an enemy's ballistic missile in its terminal phase. South Korea and America made a joint announcement on July 8th, 2016 that they agreed to deploy an American THAAD missile in South Korea.

China and Russia. I will assist Russia and Russia can survive after that. Putin can survive. Japan can also be friends with Russia. If America and Japan can both be friends with Russia, Russia will choose this direction and keep some distance from China. After that, I will attack North Korea. There needs to be separation from other greater countries. North Korea can be conquered in one month if alone. I think so. In the diplomatic meaning, I need good relationships with South Korea and Japan.

Another direction is to ask South Korea and Japan to protect themselves by nuclear weapons. North Korea is your potential enemy. So, it's your enemy, not the enemy of the United States of America. We are far from North Korea. They cannot fight against the United States. They can only attack the American base camps in places like Japan and South Korea. We will never be defeated by them.

I will, after great consideration, eventually ask South Korea and Japan to protect themselves by themselves. It's possible. If the U.S. insists that they protect themselves, this can become the world trend.

So, now is the time for Japan to change. Only the Happiness Realization Party's policy and Mr. Abe's hidden desire is to protect Japan by a stronger army.

So, I will assist in that opinion. Japan is filled with left-wing opinions of the mass media. It's very difficult for politicians to make progress in defense, so I will assist. This is your future.

8

THE SECRET OF THE GOD OF AMERICA

YUTA OKAWA

Thank you. I guess you are the highest spirit in the United States, *in Heaven*.

WASHINGTON

Uh-huh. [*Laughs.*] OK.

YUTA OKAWA

[*Laughs.*] So, I think you know God's Will about the United States and God's plan for the United States in the next several decades. Could you tell us God's next plan for the United States and this world?

WASHINGTON

It's your strong point. You are majoring in the hegemonic problem of countries. Oh, please teach me how to realize hegemony for America.

YUTA OKAWA

I think America is now having a hegemonic power, and thus, your strength will solve everything. I believe that if you were stronger than Xi Jinping and Vladimir Putin, you will realize hegemony.

WASHINGTON

Hmm, OK. That's a good point. If, IF, *if*, Ms. Hillary Clinton becomes the next president, America will lose its hegemonic power over the world. I strongly insist on this point. So, the clever American people, without mistake, will choose me as the next president. It will bring new hope for America in the 21st, 22nd and the following centuries, I think. My success will make the next 300 years of prosperity in the United States.

YUTA OKAWA

One more question. Do you have specific friends in Heaven, spirits who are either American or other nationalities?

WASHINGTON
I am the king of the United States, so no one can compare with me. Even the famous Lincoln just remade the United States. He was not the founder. He was a remaker. So, I am in a higher position than Lincoln.

ISONO
Are you the top of the American spiritual world?

WASHINGTON
No, there is the Creator.

YUTA OKAWA
Creator?

WASHINGTON
So, I'm second to the Creator.

ISONO
If possible, could you please tell us the name of the Creator?

WASHINGTON
He says, "I'm Thoth*."

ISONO
Thoth?

WASHINGTON
God Thoth.

YUTA OKAWA
OK. You were a disciple of Thoth?

WASHINGTON
He said that he was the God of the Atlantic civilization†. He said that America is a newborn Atlantic civilization. He has such kind of mission to rebuild the Atlantic civilization again. So, he might be the God of America.

YUTA OKAWA
Thank you very much.

ISONO
So, may I ask what is the name of God you believed in

---

* A great spiritual leader who built the golden age of the Atlantic civilization around 12,000 years ago. He was known as the god of wisdom in ancient Egypt, and is also the branch spirit of the God of the Earth, El Cantare.

† A civilization that prospered on Atlantis in the Atlantic Ocean. Twelve thousand years ago, the Omniscient and Omnipotent Lord Thoth led Atlantis to the golden age, but the continent sank underwater 10,400 years ago. Refer to *The Laws of the Sun* (Ryuho Okawa, [New York: IRH Press, 2013]).

while you were alive? Was it God Thoth?

WASHINGTON

Hmm?

ISONO

Oh, I mean...

WASHINGTON

Ah, no, no, no, no. When I was living in the flesh, I was a Christian and of course believed in Jesus Christ. Through Jesus Christ, I believed in his Father. But I didn't know the name of our Father. Now, I know Him.

ISONO

OK. Historically, you were not only a Christian but also a member of Freemasonry*.

WASHINGTON

Uh-huh. OK.

* A secret society, with approximately 6 million members around the world, that has been said to have prospered from a stonemason guild in Medieval Europe. They claim to be "a fraternal organization that seeks the self-improvement of its members and, through them, the improvement of society," but the details of their activities are not disclosed. Washington joined the Free Mason of Virginia in 1752.

ISONO

So, could you tell us about your relation with Freemasonry?

WASHINGTON

In reality, when I was a human, I didn't know clearly about the relationship between God and being a Freemason. But now, I understand that the real Grand Master of Freemasonry is God Hermes. So, I've been told God Hermes and God Thoth are the same consciousness. I've heard that the Thoth-Hermes-sovereignty* has taken leadership in these several thousand years, especially in the Western countries. So, the belief in Thoth and the belief in Hermes are not different, it's the same. I think so.

* In Ancient Egypt, there was the idea that the god of wisdom Thoth and Greek God Hermes were one entity. The concept that the entity guided Ancient Egypt was called the Thoth-Hermes-sovereignty and the entity of the two united was called "Hermes Trismegistus" (triple great Hermes). At Happy Science, it is revealed that God Thoth is the God of the Atlantic Civilization, that Hermes is the reincarnation of Thoth and that both are branch spirits of God of the Earth, El Cantare. Refer to *The Mystical Laws* (Ryuho Okawa, [Tokyo: HS Press, 2015]).

9

HIS PAST LIVES AS A GOD IN INDIA, EUROPE, AND AFRICA

YUTA OKAWA

Thank you very much. The time is nearly up, so if you have any message toward the American people, could you please tell us?

WASHINGTON

Oh, OK. My message is that I'm in the position of *Ame-no-Minakanushi** in Japan. You know, the central god of the universe. It's a good name, a big name, but I am the Ame-no-Minakanushi of Japan who was born in America. Not himself, but almost in equal position as his. So, we're friends.

YUTA OKAWA

OK, thank you very much. Yes, you are also very positive and honest.

---

* One of the central gods of Japanese Shintoism. Described in folk stories in the *Kojiki* (*Records of Ancient Matters*) as the original God. Happy Science has conducted spiritual research in the past and revealed that Yuta Okawa is the reincarnation of Ame-no-Minakanushi.

WASHINGTON

Positive, yeah, of course. I'm positive, I have originality and I like creation. Yeah, that's the reason.

YUTA OKAWA

I feel an affinity between us. Thank you very much.

ISONO

If I may ask, could you tell us about your reincarnations or past lives?

WASHINGTON

Past lives?

ISONO

Yes, before you were born as George Washington. Who were you?

WASHINGTON

Ah...it's very difficult to say because I'm the original god of the United States of America. If I say I was born in another country, the American people will be very sad about that. So, it's very difficult, but if I can say a little, I was one of the gods of India, one of the gods of Europe and one of the gods of Africa. I can say that.

YUTA OKAWA

Indian god? We know a lot of names of Indian gods. God Shiva[*]? Am I right?

WASHINGTON

Ah, Shiva. Umm…is it a good meaning or not? Not Shiva, but the role is a little similar to Shiva.

YUTA OKAWA

Indra[†]?

WASHINGTON

Indra? Hmm. Indra, Indra...I have another name, but how should I say...It's OK. It's about India, but I'm American, so don't worry.

ISONO

Then, let's keep it a secret of yours.

---

[*] One of the highest gods of Hinduism. God that controls destruction.

[†] A god of Hinduism. The Sakra devanam Indra of Buddhism.

WASHINGTON

Anyway, I was the founder of a country or civilization, or a big name in the period of prosperity of a civilization. I was in the same situation as Ame-no-Minakanushi in Japan. The American people should know his name. "Yuta Okawa is equal to George Washington. So, from now on, he will spread the new Truth to the United States. You should follow him."

10

DECLARING HIS REBIRTH AS DONALD TRUMP

ISONO

And now, you are born as Mr. Donald Trump.

YUTA OKAWA

Donald Trump.

WASHINGTON

Oh, yeah.

ISONO

So, you are the next president.

WASHINGTON

But I'm old. I'm 70 years old, so I don't have enough time. I can only be a president for eight years. You have 50 years until you become my age, so you have enough time.

YUTA OKAWA

Thank you very much. I need to strive.

ISONO

OK, once again, could you give a message to the American people?

WASHINGTON

Americans, please vote for me.

[*Interviewers laugh.*]

YUTA OKAWA

OK, OK.

ISONO
Is that all?

WASHINGTON
Yeah, that's all…

ISONO
OK, thank you very…

WASHINGTON
…and depend on me. Rely on me, rely on me, rely on me.

YUTA OKAWA
OK.

WASHINGTON
That's everything.

ISONO
Everything, OK.

WASHINGTON
Don't choose Hillary.

YUTA OKAWA
We respect your message.

WASHINGTON
It will mean America's death.

YUTA OKAWA
OK, OK. Thank you very much.

ISONO
Thank you very much for a wonderful lecture.

WASHINGTON
Thank you. [*Claps once.*]

RYUHO OKAWA
Hai [Japanese word for OK].

ISONO
Thank you very much, Master Ryuho Okawa.

RYUHO OKAWA
Hai.

[*Audience applaud.*]

Chapter 4

THE TRUMP CARD *in the* UNITED STATES

Spiritual Messages from the Guardian Spirit of Donald Trump

Held January 5, 2016
Happy Science General Headquarters, Tokyo

We, Japanese, are looking for a strong America.

Here, we've found a strong new U.S. president-to-be through

"Spiritual Interview with the Guardian Spirit of Donald Trump".

I hope he (Mr. Donald Trump) will be a great new leader of the U.S.

And, I, myself, want to believe his honesty, bravery, and friendship.

We expect him to succeed in diplomacy and economic policy.

May God save America and the world!

Ryuho Okawa
Master and CEO of Happy Science Group
January 11, 2016

From the Preface given for the book, Shugorei Interview Donald Trump America Fukkatsu eno Senryaku [*Spiritual Interview with the Guardian Spirit of Donald Trump - The Strategy to Rebuild the United States*] (*Tokyo: IRH Press, 2016*).

Donald Trump (1946 - Present)

The 45th president of the United States [expected to take office in January 2017].

Born in New York City. After graduating from the University of Pennsylvania in 1968, he began to work at his father's real estate company and was given control of the company in 1971. Caught the media's attention upon completing the Trump Tower on Fifth Avenue in New York in 1983, a building some people call to be the most expensive in the world. Trump is known as a real estate magnate, making millions and billions due to his great success in real estate development and hotel and casino management. His autobiography published when he was 41 years old became a bestseller. Trump has works on success theory and has been making many appearances in the media.

Trump made his presidential announcement in June 2015. He had caused a great controversy in the media through his remarks against immigrants and other issues. In July 2016, Trump was selected as the winner of the Republican Party presidential primaries, and in the November presidential election, he defeated Hillary Clinton of the Democratic Party to become the next president.

Interviewers from Happy Science*:

Yuki Oikawa
Director of Foreign Affairs
Happiness Realization Party

Masashi Ishikawa
Director General of International Editorial Division

Mariko Isis
Vice Chairperson of the Board of Directors
Supervisor of International Headquarters

This chapter is the transcript of spiritual messages given in English by the guardian spirit of Mr. Donald Trump. These spiritual messages were channeled through Ryuho Okawa by his extraordinary spiritual power. The opinions of the spirits do not necessarily reflect those of Happy Science Group. For the mechanism behind spiritual messages, see end section.

---

* Interviewers are listed in the order that they appear in the transcript. Their professional titles represent their positions at the time of the interview.

1

THE GUARDIAN SPIRIT OF "THE NEXT PRESIDENT" TRUMP APPEARS

RYUHO OKAWA

I'll invite the guardian spirit of Mr. Donald Trump, the famous candidate running for the U.S. presidency. He's a very difficult person, I guess. He has a lot of techniques to get the heart of the people, so you must be careful and watchful. Please see through his real mind from your accurate questions.

I guess he, himself, intends to make this a big chance for himself to get Japanese support for his presidency, so be careful with your questions.

This is his autobiography, *Trump: The Art of the Deal*. It was originally published in 1987 and its translation was sold in Japan the next year, in 1988. At the time, he was a very handsome person at only 42 and already had 400 billion yen. He was very handsome at that time. Now, I don't know [*laughs*], but he used to be.

Today's aim is to get his real thinking and real attitude, for example, on international politics, Japan, Japanese people, Okinawa, China, Russia and Islamic people. We must learn from his guardian spirit what he really believes.

OK? Then, we will start, but he's a bit difficult, so be careful. Please be strong. OK? [*Claps hands three times.*] Then, I'll invite him. [*Claps hands once.*]

The guardian spirit of Mr. Donald Trump, would you come down here? We want to ask you several questions. Mr. Donald Trump, the candidate for the U.S. presidency, Donald Trump, would you come down here? This is Happy Science General Headquarters in Tokyo.

[*Summons his guardian spirit.*]
[*About 10 seconds of silence.*]

I'm Trump, but not a candidate

DONALD TRUMP'S GUARDIAN SPIRIT
Hmm…

YUKI OIKAWA
Mr. Trump?

TRUMP'S GUARDIAN SPIRIT
Oh?

OIKAWA
Thank you for...

TRUMP'S GUARDIAN SPIRIT
Oh, you speak English. OK, OK. Not so bad. Hmm.

OIKAWA
Thank you very much for joining us today. Do you realize that you were invited to Happy Science General Headquarters in Japan?

TRUMP'S GUARDIAN SPIRIT
Huh? Huh? What?

OIKAWA
Do you realize that you were invited to Happy Science General Headquarters?

TRUMP'S GUARDIAN SPIRIT
What do you mean by "realize"?

OIKAWA
Are you aware of where you are?

TRUMP'S GUARDIAN SPIRIT
You just called me, so I came here. I'm Donald Trump, but I'm not a *candidate* for the presidency. I'm the *next president*, you know? Please call me, "The Next President, Mr. Trump." It's the formal standard. OK?

OIKAWA
Yes, OK. This is your opportunity to have your spiritual interview through Master Ryuho Okawa here. You can just relax, because we are not attacking you. We are not CNN or NBC.

TRUMP'S GUARDIAN SPIRIT
Really? Sneak attack, I can guess.

OIKAWA
We are not that kind of people.

TRUMP'S GUARDIAN SPIRIT
Oh, really?

2

THE TRUE INTENTION IN THE VIOLENT REMARKS AGAINST IMMIGRANTS

I, myself, am an advertisement

OIKAWA
Now, we would like to ask you several questions, OK?

TRUMP'S GUARDIAN SPIRIT
OK. Are you a good man?

OIKAWA
Yes, I am. We all are. Thank you, Mr. Trump. Here's the first question. You were divisive force in U.S. politics last year by a succession of discriminatory remarks against Mexicans, women and Muslims.

TRUMP'S GUARDIAN SPIRIT
You are an enemy [*audience laugh*].

OIKAWA
OK. However. However, you faced many criticisms and you got a huge media coverage. Even so, your rating is

still very high and you are a frontrunner.

TRUMP'S GUARDIAN SPIRIT
Frontrunner? No, next president [*audience laugh*].

OIKAWA
OK. Did your success so far and people's reactions to your blunt attitude and style surprise you or not?

TRUMP'S GUARDIAN SPIRIT
Hmm… What's the problem? I can't understand. I'm very popular in the United States. You, the Japanese, don't know my real popularity. So, I can't understand your first question. Criminality?

OIKAWA
Discrimination.

TRUMP'S GUARDIAN SPIRIT
Discrimination!? Oh, no, no, no. I'm a person of love for the world! You misunderstood me already. I just said on behalf of a small portion of people of the United States; people who hate such kind of illegal people living in the United States that insist a lot of rights without paying taxes. I just represented such an opinion through my

mouth, so it's not my real idea. I just checked it.

OIKAWA

Master Ryuho Okawa talked about your technique before this interview. Are you using any other advertising techniques in your campaign?

TRUMP'S GUARDIAN SPIRIT

Oh, no, no, no. I, myself, am an advertisement, so I don't need any advertising. I, myself, am advertising. I am the Trump Tower itself. I, myself, am very famous. So, I don't need any technique.

OIKAWA

You are always honest? Is that what you mean?

TRUMP'S GUARDIAN SPIRIT

Oh, yeah, yeah. Honesty is my best virtue, I think. Honesty is the best. Honesty is the best way to get money and succeed in business.

Japan should be the one to open up And accept immigrants

OIKAWA

More recently, you have said you would stop immigration for those of the Muslim faith and deport many Muslims from your country. Is that what you are planning to do when you become the president?

TRUMP'S GUARDIAN SPIRIT

It's a great task of the American president. Islamic immigrants are a very important matter. I'm honest, so I fought this matter. It's not good in terms of populism, but I'm honest.

I'm not Hitler. I'm quite opposite to Hitler. So I, myself, warned against them. If they all come to the United States in my presidency, they will suffer a lot of problems. I already warned them. So, I'm not Hitler. I am more conscientious. I have more conscience regarding immigrants.

But immigration is a deep, deep problem in the U.S., so you, the Japanese, don't know about that. You already keep a closed-door policy in Japan, so you have no right to criticize me about that!

OIKAWA
Do you have any suggestions to the Japanese people or government?

TRUMP'S GUARDIAN SPIRIT
Open! Open your country. Open your country.

OIKAWA
Accept more people from other countries?

TRUMP'S GUARDIAN SPIRIT
Yeah! It's your obligation. Please accept all the immigrants who are suffering from the war of the Islamic matter. You must accept the Syrian people and the people who are living in Iraq and the Islamic State. You are responsible for that. I think so.

MASASHI ISHIKAWA
Excuse me.

TRUMP'S GUARDIAN SPIRIT
OK!

ISHIKAWA

So, you mean the Japanese population is decreasing and that's why we need to accept immigrants?

TRUMP'S GUARDIAN SPIRIT

OK. OK.

ISHIKAWA

But the American population is increasing, so you don't have to accept immigrants? Do you mean it like that? No? Is it our responsibility?

TRUMP'S GUARDIAN SPIRIT

Hmm… I don't know your problem of a decreasing population, but you have money for such kind of poor and miserable people. If you have a lot of mercy, please accept these people. In America, we are already suffering from a lot of discrimination. We have been struggling, but you've never experienced such kind of problem. So, if you are the top runner of the countries worldwide, you must experience such a problem. It will be your test as the leader of the world.

ISHIKAWA

So, America is a great nation…

TRUMP'S GUARDIAN SPIRIT

Yeah. Indeed.

ISHIKAWA

...that has accepted many immigrants so far.

TRUMP'S GUARDIAN SPIRIT

America has Donald Trump. This is the certification of a great country. [*Laughs.*]

3

ON THE CRITICISMS FROM THE MASS MEDIA

ISHIKAWA

I heard that your campaign slogan is, "Make America Great Again."

TRUMP'S GUARDIAN SPIRIT

Oh, yeah, yeah, yeah.

ISHIKAWA

This slogan is the same as that of Ronald Reagan, I think...

TRUMP'S GUARDIAN SPIRIT

Ronald Reagan? I hate him. I hate him.

ISHIKAWA

Really? I thought you respected him... Do you really hate him?

TRUMP'S GUARDIAN SPIRIT

He is poor in mind. In reality, he had some problem in his head during his presidency. He was an actor, so he played as the president, but he was not a real president.

ISHIKAWA

Oh, really? I thought he was a great hero in the Republican Party.

TRUMP'S GUARDIAN SPIRIT

No, no, no, no, no, no, no. He pretended to be a great leader of the Republicans. I have real power, real knowledge, real activity and real capability to become an American president. The first and the last president of America.

Criticism is a New York cheesecake

ISHIKAWA
This is Mr. Yuta's request. He is Master Okawa's son. The mass media always exaggerate your comments badly and as a result, you are criticized a lot. Maybe you don't mind these criticisms, but what do you think about their mindset? Is it evil or…

TRUMP'S GUARDIAN SPIRIT
It's just because I'm strong. That's the reason. I'm strong. Hmm.

ISHIKAWA
So, no problem, then?

TRUMP'S GUARDIAN SPIRIT
No problem. I'm strong.

OIKAWA
So, you are not afraid of criticisms from the mass media?

TRUMP'S GUARDIAN SPIRIT
I'm not afraid of any criticisms. I am the strongest president. Hmm. I think so.

ISHIKAWA
But you said…

TRUMP'S GUARDIAN SPIRIT
I already am the president.

ISHIKAWA
So, you are special, then.

TRUMP'S GUARDIAN SPIRIT
Obama, "the black angel from Hell," is already dead.

OIKAWA
Maybe the other politicians in the U.S. are afraid of criticisms by the press.

TRUMP'S GUARDIAN SPIRIT
Oh, really?

OIKAWA
But you are so tough. How?

TRUMP'S GUARDIAN SPIRIT

Because…

OIKAWA

Are you using the power of the press?

TRUMP'S GUARDIAN SPIRIT

Criticism is my favorite. It's a sweet dessert for me. When you want a cup of coffee, you want some cake or something like that, right? For me, criticism is a New York cheesecake.

ISHIKAWA

I think you said politicians should be cautious about dealing with the mass media. But you are special, you are different. Ordinary politicians should be cautious.

TRUMP'S GUARDIAN SPIRIT

For me, criticism is an advertisement in disguise. Every criticism will be advertising for me because I'm strong. I'm confident of my ability!

4

BEING HONEST APPEARS AS DISCRIMINATION AGAINST WOMEN

MARIKO ISIS

Yes. I can feel that from you, as I see you on TV.

TRUMP'S GUARDIAN SPIRIT

Ah, a beautiful lady.

ISIS

Thank you so much. You're looking nice, too.

TRUMP'S GUARDIAN SPIRIT

Why are you sitting there? You're young, beautiful and clever.

ISIS

[*Laughs.*] Thank you so much. Many people criticize you...

TRUMP'S GUARDIAN SPIRIT

Oh? Really? I don't know. I don't know.

ISIS

...saying that you are discriminating against women. But as I see you in a lot of TV programs, I feel that you're just an honest man.

TRUMP'S GUARDIAN SPIRIT

Honest man. Yeah, yeah. That's right.

ISIS

You're just honest, too honest.

TRUMP'S GUARDIAN SPIRIT

Too honest!

ISIS

If you think that a woman doesn't look good, you just say it, right?

TRUMP'S GUARDIAN SPIRIT

[*Taps on the cover of his autobiography with his portrait on it.*]

[*Audience laugh.*]

TRUMP'S GUARDIAN SPIRIT
Nice young man. Used to be.

ISIS
Yes, you do look good. Well, I wanted to ask you, do you intend to do that or does your mouth just slip? Are you just honest? Or, are you using the mass media to be rude? Are you intending to be rude?

TRUMP'S GUARDIAN SPIRIT
OK, OK, OK, OK, OK, OK.

ISIS
Most people think that you're rude. But I just think you're honest.

I'm giving meat to hungry lions

TRUMP'S GUARDIAN SPIRIT
I appreciate your friendship very much. I appreciate you, but the mass media have their business. They need a lot of articles to write, so they want articles every day. They are hungry. They are hungry lions, I mean. The reality of the mass media is that they are hungry lions. Hungry

lions need meat. A lot of raw meat. So, I, myself, want to give them meat.

ISIS
So, you're doing an act of love.

TRUMP'S GUARDIAN SPIRIT
To give.

ISIS
To give them more meat.

TRUMP'S GUARDIAN SPIRIT
Yeah. So, they can write about me, earn money and make a living. It's my love for them. I love the mass media very much.

ISIS
Yes, and as a result of that, you are loved much more by men than women because you are just honest. But I think that is the reason why you are popular.

5

VIEWS ON JAPAN-U.S. TIES, JAPAN-SOUTH KOREA TIES, RUSSIA, IRAN AND CHINA

Japan should shut up If it cannot protect itself

ISIS

And I wanted to ask you another question about the U.S.-Japan Security Treaty.

TRUMP'S GUARDIAN SPIRIT

Security Treaty?

ISIS

Yes. You said that it is unfair…

TRUMP'S GUARDIAN SPIRIT

Unfair, unfair. Unfair is a good…

ISIS

…for the United States to have to go and save Japan when Japan is in danger, but the Japanese people don't have to save Americans.

TRUMP'S GUARDIAN SPIRIT
I hate the Okinawan people. We, the American army, are protecting Japan from the enemies of Japan, but they hate us, do a lot of demonstrations and say, "Yankee, go home." And there is the Henoko problem in Okinawa. If they want to do so, please protect it by yourselves. Please have nuclear weapons in Japan. If you cannot do that, then shut up, Japanese! Shut up, Okinawa!

ISIS
So, if you become the president, you are going to say that?

TRUMP'S GUARDIAN SPIRIT
I'm already the president.

ISIS
Yes, OK.

TRUMP'S GUARDIAN SPIRIT
Virtually. In the supernatural world.

South Korea must be Respectful toward Japan

ISIS

OK. And as South Korea is near Japan, what do you think about South Korea? Last year, South Korea and Japan reached an agreement on the comfort women issue*.

TRUMP'S GUARDIAN SPIRIT

Ah, comfort women issue. No, no.

ISIS

Can you tell us what you think of Japan and South Korea?

TRUMP'S GUARDIAN SPIRIT

I don't know the real facts, but it's not recommendable for the dignity of the Korean people. It's rude. It will make many difficulties between South Korea and Japan.

South Korea has a very difficult emotion about Japan, I know. The historical fact… I don't really understand the old history and its real fact, but as a businessman, the Korean attitude is not so good for business partner-

---

* On December 28, 2015, the Japanese and South Korean governments agreed to "a final and irreversible" resolution regarding the comfort women issue.

ship, so they will get worse and worse in economy.

Ms. Park, the president, made a great mistake, I guess. "Japan was a bad country"—all the people of the world thought so 70 years ago, but now, Japan is one of the countries leading the world, so they must have some kind of respectful attitude toward Japan. It's the middle way, I think. But this problem is very difficult.

It's a very difficult matter, so I cannot say decisive things. But if Korean people want to become happier, they should abandon such kind of opinion. They are bad in their attitude. They want to belong to the U.S., China, Japan or North Korea. They are wavering now, so they must be serious about their future.

OIKAWA

I'm very surprised. You seem to like Japan.

TRUMP'S GUARDIAN SPIRIT

Yeah, of course, of course! I like *geisha* and *fuji-yama* [*audience laugh*]. Geisha, fuji-yama and Happy Science. I like… I love them.

OIKAWA

But in your campaign, you criticized Japan. You attacked Japan over the international trade.

TRUMP'S GUARDIAN SPIRIT
Small point, small point. It's a very small point. OK? I love Japan, of course.

If I were Putin, I would do something this year

OIKAWA
OK. Moving on to the Russian problem. About the Russian president. Since the Ukrainian crisis two years ago, American politicians like Obama, Hillary and everybody else criticized and said, "Putin is the modern Hitler." However, you said Putin is the only effective leader in the world.* Why are you so comfortable praising him?

TRUMP'S GUARDIAN SPIRIT
He has real leadership and he can make decisions. He is a real power holder, I think. In some meaning, I respect him.

It's very difficult to say, but if I were in his place, I would do something this year, 2016, because there is Obama in America. The presidency of Obama is weak.

---

* Trump's statement made in a TV show on December 18, 2015.

The weakest president, so Putin can do everything. Before my presidency, he can do everything. This is a very difficult year for the U.S., but a very good year for Russia. He is the world leader now, but next year, I will be the strongest person in the world. So, only this year, you must be careful and be wise.

OIKAWA
If you really become the U.S. president, will you allow the Japanese government to be friendly with the Russian government?

TRUMP'S GUARDIAN SPIRIT
The Japanese government and the Russian government?

OIKAWA
We have a territorial dispute.

TRUMP'S GUARDIAN SPIRIT
Ah, a small dispute. It's a very small one. Please forget about it. If you want your four small islands and want to solve this problem, please buy the Siberian district from Russia. You can. They need money.

China's plan is complicating things In the Middle East

ISHIKAWA

Last year, Western countries and Iran reached a landmark deal on Iran's nuclear problem*.

TRUMP'S GUARDIAN SPIRIT

[*Sighs.*]

ISHIKAWA

And yesterday, Saudi Arabia cut diplomatic ties with Iran. So, what do you think about this kind of...

TRUMP'S GUARDIAN SPIRIT

Maybe it's regarding oil price or oil money. Saudi Arabian economy is not so good. Ten trillion yen deficit, they say. I don't know the problem exactly, but maybe Iran and Saudi Arabia would be the next problem. I mean in this area in the Middle East, there is Russia, America, Japan and the Chinese power colliding, so it's very difficult.

---

*In July 2015, the UN Security Council endorsed a joint comprehensive agreement on Iran's nuclear program.

The most difficult problem is the Chinese plan. They want to make a new Silk Road. It will be their next target. I mean the starting point of the Third World War.

ISHIKAWA
During the Obama administration, the U.S. is stepping down from the role of policing the world.

TRUMP'S GUARDIAN SPIRIT
No, no, no, no, no. Not yet. I'm the next president, so not yet.

6

WHAT WOULD HILLARY BRING AS THE PRESIDENT?

ISHIKAWA
I think you said Hillary Clinton was the worst secretary of state in the history of the country*. Maybe you need to confront Hillary Clinton, so...

* Trump's repeated statement since July 2015.

TRUMP'S GUARDIAN SPIRIT

Because she is the worst wife of the worst president, Clinton. Why did Mr. Clinton's wife... Hmm... Argh... Bad president! Mr. Clinton was a bad president. And at that time, his adviser was Hillary. It's incredible! She's not a lady! Just an old person! Oh... did I say something wrong? Oh...

ISIS

I think it's OK.

TRUMP'S GUARDIAN SPIRIT

OK, OK. All right, all right.

ISIS

You said that Obama and Hillary created ISIS and you're going to cut ISIS' head off*. I think this is your biggest thing that you're claiming. How are you going to do that? I just wanted to ask. Do you have any plans?

TRUMP'S GUARDIAN SPIRIT

Hmm... Obama has made a lot of deficit for our country, so it's the fault of the Democratic Party. How should I

* Trump's statement made in his first campaign commercial, aired starting January 4, 2016.

deal with this matter? It's very difficult, but I can predict at this point that if Hillary, Hillary "Clinton" becomes the next president, it'll be the end of the world!

ISIS
But how do you think the world will end?

TRUMP'S GUARDIAN SPIRIT
Because America would not be America at that time. America would be one of the ladies' countries. It would be famous for having a lady president. That's all. So, nothing powerful. No ability to consult or to resolve the world's problems. I mean… she is not a decisive person, just a housewife. Oh! [*Audience laugh.*] Was that a misfire? A misfire? Oh, I don't know.

OIKAWA
If you run against Hillary Clinton in a general election, according to the current polls, media expect that you would lose badly because of your unpopularity with women. So, how are you going to compete with Hillary? Do you have any hidden cards?

TRUMP'S GUARDIAN SPIRIT
Woah… You misunderstood me. [*In a low, soft voice*]

I'm a very sexy person, so I'm very welcomed by women. They are apt to hide their real sympathy for me. I'm a magician that controls women's emotions, you know?

OIKAWA
Then, are you going to show how much you love women?

TRUMP'S GUARDIAN SPIRIT
I have a lot of experience, so I can. Yes, I can. Yes, we can. Yes, I'll challenge!

OIKAWA
So, you are sure that you will attract women's votes?

TRUMP'S GUARDIAN SPIRIT
OK, OK, OK. No problem. I'm an experienced person, so no problem.

7

RECOVERING THE U.S. ECONOMY

I'm an expert in economy Who receives inspiration from Heaven

ISHIKAWA
I think now, the world and America need a strong leader like you.

TRUMP'S GUARDIAN SPIRIT
Yeah, yeah, yeah.

ISHIKAWA
Especially, republican voters are frustrated with existing politicians. So, they look for an outsider like you…

TRUMP'S GUARDIAN SPIRIT
"Outsider like you"?

ISHIKAWA
Oh, sorry. A new politician, a new leader like you. Actually, some people criticize you saying that you have no achievement, no career as a politician.

But in the business world, you are a real estate tycoon

and you have a great achievement in the business world, so maybe you can make use of these skills in the political world. What do you think about these criticisms that say you have no career as a politician?

TRUMP'S GUARDIAN SPIRIT

This final year of the Obama presidency, he will make a new bubble [burst]. I will make the U.S. recover from its recession, starting next year.

So, please rely on me. He will make the final disaster for the American people this year. The American bubble, you know? It's a bubble. America's economy is not good, but he thinks the economy is becoming better and better. But it's an illusion. It's a bubble.

ISHIKAWA

Last year [December 2015], Chairman of FRB, Yellen, raised the interest rate.

TRUMP'S GUARDIAN SPIRIT

It's a misjudgment. It's a mistake in decision. American economy is bad, very bad.

ISHIKAWA

Maybe this year, she will raise the interest rate three times or four times.

TRUMP'S GUARDIAN SPIRIT

No, it's a mistake. Our economy is not so good. It's near the next great fall.

ISHIKAWA

So, the unemployment rate is decreasing, but it's not a good decision?

TRUMP'S GUARDIAN SPIRIT

I, myself, am an expert in economy and of course a great businessman, so I know everything. I especially receive some kind of inspiration from Heaven about the economy, so my inspiration is 100 percent correct! Please rely on me.

The new force regarding business

ISHIKAWA

I have one more question on economic policies. Pfizer,

one of the biggest drug companies, tried to move its headquarters from the U.S. to Ireland because America's corporate tax rate is very high at about 40 percent, whereas Ireland's corporate tax rate is very low. These kinds of problems occur in America frequently, so Hillary said that America needs to solve these kinds of problems. What do you think about these tax rate issues?

TRUMP'S GUARDIAN SPIRIT

Uh-huh. Hmm… [*Claps his hands a few times.*] Economic growth is first, I think. It comes first. And next is [to resolve] financial deficit, I think. Japan must obey this rule. If Mr. Abe, the Japanese prime minister, chooses to deal with financial deficit first and then economic growth, he will fail in the recovery of the Japanese economy.

ISHIKAWA

So, even in America, you think you need to decrease the corporate tax rate?

TRUMP'S GUARDIAN SPIRIT

Hmm… maybe. Maybe. May… be!

OIKAWA

What about the individual income tax rate?

TRUMP'S GUARDIAN SPIRIT

Individual income tax... I hate communism-like equality because wealth is for the people who earn money by themselves and for themselves. I, myself, made a lot of wealth. But it's not unfair, I think. It's just based on my thinking method and my efforts.

You already know that "think big" is a great method. I, myself, experienced that "think big" attitude is the acceleration for personal business grade-up. How to find the balance between "think big" and "be careful" is the crucial point of real management. I did and I could do so. This is my starting point.

In the financial meaning, I'm a great person and a wealthy person. But to become wealthy, personally, we need the attitude of "think big" and at the same time, of "be careful." These two things are very difficult. Very easy to say, but very difficult to carry out. So, these kinds of personal efforts are required for every American businessman and businesswoman. It's the new meaning of the "business force." I think so.

I want to encourage such kind of people who have

this new force regarding business. So, it's very difficult to just say, "lower taxes or higher taxes." It's easy to say, but it's difficult. If I make a mistake in my judgment, it will be communitarian-like thinking.

I want to keep cultivating the American economic growth power and cherish those who carry out such kind of attitude. I respect such kind of people and I want to help such kind of people. I'm quite different from communitarian people, so America must destroy the Democratic Party. They are almost equal to communism. I hate such kind of communism.

I believe in God

ISHIKAWA
Yeah. Actually, I think you are a very merciful person.

TRUMP'S GUARDIAN SPIRIT
Ah, yeah.

ISHIKAWA
I read your book, written with Robert Kiyosaki, the author of *Rich Dad, Poor Dad*. The title is, *Why We*

Want You to Be Rich. In America, middle-class people are very important, so I think you are very merciful and you want to get rid of poverty from this world. Maybe you are influenced by Norman Vincent Peale*.

TRUMP'S GUARDIAN SPIRIT
Ah, yeah.

ISHIKAWA
I think Norman Vincent Peale was your father's friend and pastor. So, you wrote the book, *Think Like a Billionaire*. If possible, could you tell me the key to success?

TRUMP'S GUARDIAN SPIRIT
Oh, my basic thinking and the Happy Science thinking are almost the same. I think so. That's why you, Happy Science people, should support me!

I think big, you think big. I think carefully, you think carefully. I think worldwide and you think worldwide. I believe in God and you believe in God. So, we

* Norman Vincent Peale [1898~1993] was an American minister and author. A progenitor of "positive thinking." His book, *The Power of Positive Thinking* became a bestseller, selling 20 million copies worldwide. Peale is currently one of the guiding spirits of Happy Science. His spiritual message has been published with the title, *The World of "Positive Thinking"—Spiritual Interview with N. V. Peale—* [published by Happy Science, 2015, English-Japanese bitext].

are the same. So, my success is your success. Your success is my success.

Please support me. Any money is welcome or I just want your pure heart for the God of prosperity. I'm the God of prosperity, himself. So, let's be friends. We must be friends.

8

EXPECTATIONS FOR THE MUSLIM IMMIGRANTS IN THE U.S.

ISIS

On one side, you are trying to cut off Muslim people from entering America, but on the other hand, I saw some kind of a speech that you made. You had a Q and A session with high school students in America and one student asked you that there are a lot of talented Muslim Americans in the United States, but are you not going to use their powers? Then, you said that you're going to use them if they have power and you are willing to use them in your cabinet, too. So, I think you have a generous heart... You don't have a problem with that, right?

You have a daughter who married a Jew and is now Jewish. So, I was thinking that maybe you are generous to all religions. Can I ask what kind of belief you have?

TRUMP'S GUARDIAN SPIRIT
In business, we have diversity. I mean that we must have friendship for different types of people or different people in belief, so I don't exclude Muslim people in reality.

But in America, there is a feeling about the terrorist attacks. Terrorism is the next great matter, so we must minimize that risk. So, we must be careful of their entering our country in order to protect against a great disaster.

But in reality, I don't hate Muslim people. If they can change their attitude to become friends and act like Americans, then we can be friends and become business partners. We can, of course, appoint them as, for example, my cabinet members or hire them in my company.

But one point I must point out is that they are very obstinate and they hesitate to change. America is a country of change, so a person who cannot change in the United States is not an American.

America gathered a lot of people from a lot of countries. We welcome them. We used to welcome them, but

Muslim people are very negative toward changing their life, their attitude or their thinking pattern; they don't think deeply about their appearances from the outside.

So, if they want to be Americans or people of the United States, behave like that! Then, I will accept.

But if they want to act and say like Islamic people in the Middle East, it'll be very difficult from now on because there is a danger of terrorist attacks. To protect this country from terrorism is a very important thing for the next president.

I already warned them about that because I don't want to exclude them, I don't want to kill them and I don't want to give them more burdens. So, before that, I just warned them to be careful and to think it through; if you want to come to America, be careful and change like an American. American method of thinking, American ways of living and American ways of behavior are required. At that time, we will welcome. Please believe in one sovereign God of the United States.

9

FORM A TRIANGLE OF GOD-BELIEVING COUNTRIES AND STAND AGAINST ATHEIST CHINA

The successful method for Japan

OIKAWA
Again, coming back to the U.S. economy, how do you see the U.S. economy recovering, especially this year? We have a common problem, the China issue. The Chinese economy is collapsing now. Yesterday, the Chinese market went down again. So, how do you see this year's U.S. economy?

TRUMP'S GUARDIAN SPIRIT
During the Obama period, you cannot expect anything. So, please protect your property. Please protect your Japanese yen and Japanese property.

Please rely on me. If I… no, not *if*, I *must be* the next president. In my presidency, if you, Happy Realization Party? No?

OIKAWA
Happiness Realization Party.

TRUMP'S GUARDIAN SPIRIT
Happiness Realization Party. Are you... going to be a ruling party? Is it possible? I don't know. But if your opinion and your activity prevail in this country, we will cooperate, make new leadership in the world and U.S.-Japan treaty will lead the next century. I mean, next one hundred years of prosperity will be promised. So, please believe in me and cooperate with me. That will be your successful method, I think.

Mr. Clinton and his wife used to be your enemies. They made the Chinese economy grow and gave you a lot of sufferings in the economic meaning. They are guilty, so never ever vote for Hillary Clinton. They are enemies of Japanese people. They caused the Japanese poverty, the Japanese economic debacle in the 90s. Hillary will repeat this pattern again, so please choose Donald Trump. This is the fatal point.

Protect against the next Hitler
By forming a U.S.-Japan-Germany triangle

OIKAWA
You are a close ally with Britain. They are very close to China. What do you think about that?

TRUMP'S GUARDIAN SPIRIT
They are poor now, so China showed them a lot of money. Our mother country, Great Britain, is sinking now, so it's very sad. Very sad.

But it's OK. Part of my blood is from Germany, so I rely on Germany. German people will change their attitude and mind concept to become the real leader of the EU. Japan will also change their willpower to lead the world. The U.S., Japan and Germany, these three countries will make the next triangle and lead the next economic world.

We must protect against China's hegemony. They are thinking bad things! Spratly Islands, you know? They're making an airport in the sea and they want to get the Philippines, Vietnam, Thailand and other countries. They are just thinking about the new Silk Road to the Arabian Peninsula.

But we must protect against this project because they don't believe in God. We, who believe in God, must gather our powers, control the world, lead the world and make a new world.

Donald Trump is the only one! People who can choose the next president must support me! Rely on me! I will save you! I will support you! I will cooperate with you! I like Ryuho Okawa! I like Oikawa! I like Miss Isis Mariko! And I like you [Ishikawa]! [*Audience laugh.*]

So, we are friends. Happy Science should dispatch their opinions to all the countries and change the mass media of Japan who are apt to write that Donald Trump is a very dangerous person or that he's a Hitler-like person.

No! The next Hitler is Xi Jinping! That's him! People or a person who can destroy him is the real Christ, Christ-to-be or next to Christ. OK? Don't misunderstand regarding this point.

ISHIKAWA

Then, is joining AIIB [Asia Infrastructure Investment Bank] established by China a wrong choice?

TRUMP'S GUARDIAN SPIRIT

Ah, wrong choice. Of course.

ISHIKAWA
How about TPP?

TRUMP'S GUARDIAN SPIRIT
TPP, hmm… A little bit of a problem, but Japanese beef is too strong, so this is the problem. It's a problem, a problem, a problem.

But maybe we can make some kind of adjustment. Japanese beef is too high in quality; we, Americans, cannot make such kind of good beef. It's like an American car, so this is the problem. We must persuade our farmers. It's a problem, but we can make some decision.

10

A "BIG NAME" FROM TRUMP'S PAST LIVES

ISIS
OK. I'm very honored to listen to your great speech today. Thank you so much.

Lastly, I want to ask you about your past life since you are the guardian spirit of Donald Trump.

TRUMP'S GUARDIAN SPIRIT

Of course, of course! You must ask about that!

[*Audience laugh.*]

ISIS

Yes, because you referred to God many times.

TRUMP'S GUARDIAN SPIRIT

God! Yeah, yeah.

ISIS

So, can you tell us about that?

TRUMP'S GUARDIAN SPIRIT

[*In a teasing manner*] George Washington!

ISIS

Wow...

TRUMP'S GUARDIAN SPIRIT

George Washington! George Washington! George Washington! That's me!

ISIS
Really... For real?

TRUMP'S GUARDIAN SPIRIT
For example.

ISIS
For example [*laughs*] [*audience laugh*].

TRUMP'S GUARDIAN SPIRIT
[*Laughs.*] If American people believe in past lives, I must say I was George Washington.

ISIS
You want to be like George Washington?

TRUMP'S GUARDIAN SPIRIT
No. I *was* George Washington. I was. I was.

ISIS
OK. Are there any others? Do you know Master Ryuho Okawa's past lives?

TRUMP'S GUARDIAN SPIRIT
I don't know [*laughs*]. But he's a great person, I know. I know, I know, I know. He's a great person. I feel some kind of affinity toward him. He might be my old friend.

OIKAWA
Did you know that he was working in the World Trade Center in the 1980s?

TRUMP'S GUARDIAN SPIRIT
Ah... I don't know, but I should know about that. I appreciate that and I can be his friend. We are gods, so gods can be friends [*audience laugh*].

OIKAWA
In your soul, do you have any other spiritual memories living in a different country other than the United States?

TRUMP'S GUARDIAN SPIRIT
Hmm... In the ancient times, I might have been Jewish. Maybe Jewish. And...

OIKAWA

Which time? In the time of Christ?

TRUMP'S GUARDIAN SPIRIT

Hmm... Hmm... Maybe a famous person, but we are Christians, so it's very difficult to say that because Christian people don't believe in such kind of reincarnation. I have one past life in the Jewish history. Before that, I was born as a king of Egypt. I was a king of Egypt and I made pyramids.

OIKAWA

Can you reveal the name of the king of Egypt?

TRUMP'S GUARDIAN SPIRIT

Hmm... maybe Echnaton [Akhenaten]* or a name like that, I think... You don't believe me, do you?

[*Audience laugh.*]

TRUMP'S GUARDIAN SPIRIT

OK, OK [*laughs*].

---

* A pharaoh of the 18th dynasty in ancient Egypt, 14th century BC. Known earlier as Amenhotep IV.

OIKAWA
Any experience of being a politician in your past lives?

TRUMP'S GUARDIAN SPIRIT
I have an experience of being a god.

OIKAWA
You are a spiritual person.

TRUMP'S GUARDIAN SPIRIT
Spiritual person, yeah. King, preacher and a god. At the time of the Crusades, I went from England to Jerusalem and did something. I was one of the generals at that time.

But correctly, I cannot remember. It's very difficult for a Christian person to answer you, so please forgive about the minor details. Please write about me in a good way. Your editor is very good at making stories, so I can expect that.

OIKAWA
He [Ishikawa] is the chief editor.

TRUMP'S GUARDIAN SPIRIT
Oh, really? You can make up any stories, then. It's all right. It's an option.

11

MESSAGE FOR THE PROSPERITY OF JAPAN AND THE U.S.

ISHIKAWA

I have one question. There are a lot of entrepreneurs in America and some of them may want to follow you and become American presidents in the future. So, if you…

TRUMP'S GUARDIAN SPIRIT

No chance for them.

ISHIKAWA

No chance for them [*laughs*]? I'm not sure if Mark Zuckerberg wants to be a president, but if you have some advice to young entrepreneurs…

TRUMP'S GUARDIAN SPIRIT

They should abandon that thought. I'm the next president. God decides that.

OIKAWA

This spiritual interview will be published in Japan and

also published in the U.S. soon, in English, edited by him. So, do you have any...

TRUMP'S GUARDIAN SPIRIT
Oh, it's OK! No problem! He can make up any stories, so it's OK. No problem.

OIKAWA
OK. Finally, do you have any last message to the Japanese people and to U.S. citizens?

TRUMP'S GUARDIAN SPIRIT
Last message?

I like U.S. citizens, of course, I like the Japanese people and I like the Islamic people. In the end, I like all the people of the world.

So, please believe in me. I like Jesus Christ. I love Jesus Christ and Jesus Christ likes Ryuho Okawa, so we are friends.

We have the same aim and the same mission. I am the savior of the United States. If the United States becomes greater and greater, Japan will prosper for more than one hundred years. So, please rely on me. We should be friends. OK?

OIKAWA

Great. Thank you very much.

ISIS

Thank you so much.

TRUMP'S GUARDIAN SPIRIT

You [Oikawa] are a good person. American people will like you. You should appear on TV, on radio or on newspapers in America. No Japanese person can speak English fluently like you. You can. Yes, you can. You can support me. You can. You should take that challenge.

OIKAWA

Thank you very much, but I have to be very careful about your humor. OK, thank you very much.

TRUMP'S GUARDIAN SPIRIT

[*Applauses as he laughs.*]

After the spiritual interview

RYUHO OKAWA

OK. He is a nice guy. I think if he were this kind of young person [cover photo of his autobiography], he could have been like John F. Kennedy. He could have gotten more popularity. He missed out on that point, but he's a good man, I think.

America should change from Democrat to Republican. It's time. Then it will help us from China's intrusion. I think so. I can persuade him. Islamic matter is a very difficult one, but we must do something about that, so we'll do our best to make a new age. He's a good person, I guess so.

Thank you. [*Claps hands twice.*]

ABOUT THE AUTHOR

RYUHO OKAWA is Global Visionary, a renowned spiritual leader, and an international best-selling author with a simple goal: to help people find true happiness and create a better world.

His deep compassion and sense of responsibility for the happiness of each individual has prompted him to publish over 2,100 titles of religious, spiritual, and self-development teachings, covering a broad range of topics including how our thoughts influence reality, the nature of love, and the path to enlightenment. He also writes on the topics of management and economy, as well as the relationship between religion and politics in the global context.

To date, Master Okawa's books have sold over 100 million copies worldwide and been translated into 28 languages. In addition to publishing books, he continues to give lectures around the world.

Furthermore, Master Okawa is giving increasing impact on a worldwide level, both through live broadcast and TV programs. From August to September of 2016, FOX5 TV aired eight episodes of his lectures in New York, New Jersey, Connecticut and Pennsylvania, inviting many positive feedbacks.

For more about Master Okawa, visit ryuho-okawa.com

Lecture Broadcasted in Over 3,500 Places Around the World

Since he established Happy Science in 1986, Master Ryuho Okawa has given more than 2,500 lectures. This photo is from the Celebration of Lord's Descent Lecture Event held at Saitama Super Arena in Japan, on July 6, 2016. In the lecture titled, "The Light That Will Save the Earth," Master spoke on the points such as the difference between revolution and terrorism, how the U.S. has been pondering about world justice, how the mass media has violated citizen rights, and the holy mission that religions must fulfill. Master Okawa closed the lecture with a powerful statement: "right religion establishes world justice and teaches people how to discern good from evil." The audience responded with a standing ovation. About 18,000 people attended the main stadium and the event was also broadcasted live in over 3,500 places around the world.

Over 2,100 Books Published

Master Ryuho Okawa's books have been translated into 28 languages and the readership is growing around the world. In 2010, he received a Guinness World Record for publishing 52 books in a year and in 2013, he published 106 books within a year. As of August 2016, the number of books published reached 2,100.

Among them there are also a lot of spiritual messages from the spirits of historical greats and the guardian spirits of important figures living in the current world.

WHAT IS A SPIRITUAL MESSAGE?

We are all spiritual beings living on this earth. The following is the mechanism behind Master Ryuho Okawa's spiritual messages.

1 You are a spirit

People are born into this world to gain wisdom through various experiences and return to the other world when their lives end. We are all spirits and repeat this cycle in order to refine our souls.

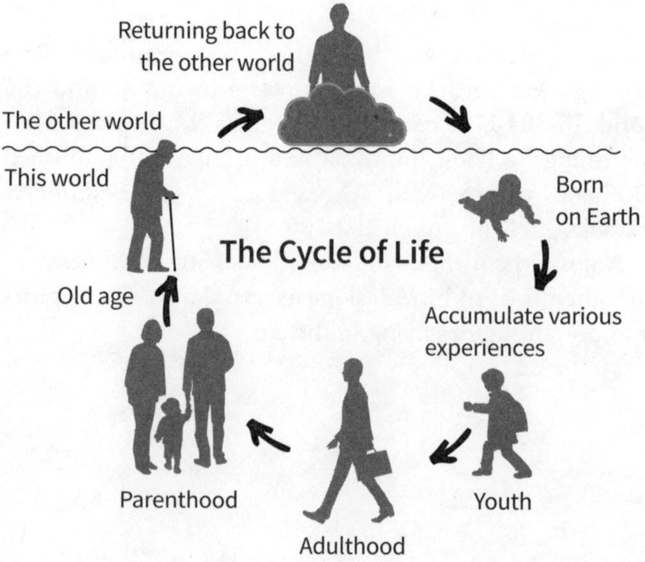

2 You have a guardian spirit

Guardian spirits are those who protect the people who are living on this earth. Each of us has a guardian spirit that watches over us and guides us from the other world. They were us in our past life, and are identical in how we think.

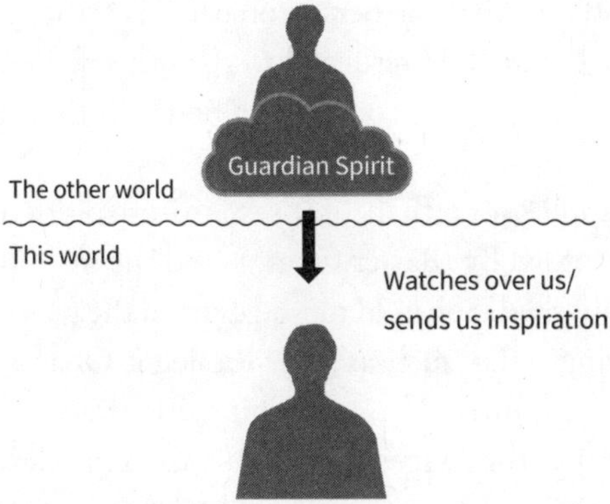

3 How spiritual messages work

Master Ryuho Okawa, through his enlightenment, is capable of summoning any spirit from anywhere in the world, including the spirit world.

Master Okawa's way of receiving spiritual messages is fundamentally different from that of other psychic mediums who undergo trances and are thereby completely taken over by the spirits they are channeling. Master Okawa's attainment of a high level of enlightenment enables him to retain full control of his consciousness and body throughout the duration of the spiritual message. To allow the spirits to express their own thoughts and personalities freely, however, Master Okawa usually softens the dominancy of his consciousness. This way, he is able to keep his own philosophies out of the way and ensure that the spiritual messages are pure expressions of the spirits he is channeling.

Since guardian spirits think at the same subconscious level as the person living on earth, Master Okawa can summon the spirit and find out what the person on earth is actually thinking. If the person has already returned to the other world, the spirit can give messages to the people living on earth through Master Okawa.

Since 2009, more than 600 sessions of spiritual messages have been recorded by Master Okawa, and the majority of these have been published. Spiritual messages from the guardian spirits of people living today such as U.S. President Obama, Japanese Prime Minister Shinzo Abe and Chinese President Xi Jinping, as well as spiritual messages sent from the spirit world by Jesus Christ, Muhammad, Thomas Edison, Mother Teresa, Steve Jobs and Nelson Mandela are just a tiny pack of spiritual messages that were published so far.

Domestically, in Japan, these spiritual messages are being read by a wide range of politicians and mass media, and the high-level contents of these books are delivering an impact even more on politics, news and public opinion. In recent years, there have been spiritual messages recorded in English, and English translations are being done on the spiritual messages given in Japanese. These have been published overseas, one after another, and have started to shake the world.

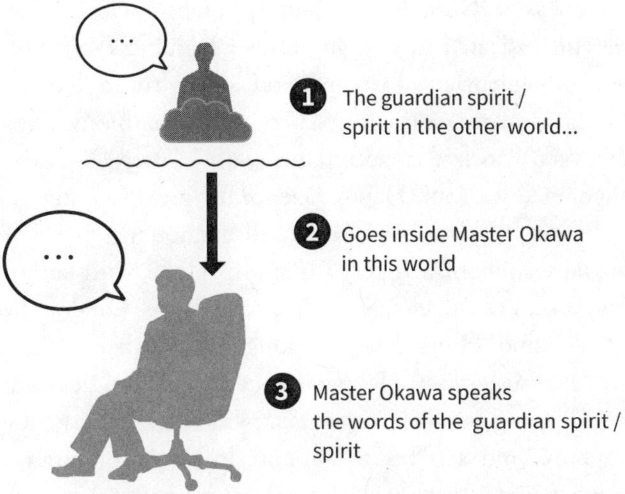
...
...
1 The guardian spirit / spirit in the other world...
2 Goes inside Master Okawa in this world
3 Master Okawa speaks the words of the guardian spirit / spirit

For more about spiritual messages and a complete list of books in the Spiritual Interview Series, visit okawabooks.com

ABOUT HAPPY SCIENCE

In 1986, Master Ryuho Okawa founded Happy Science, a spiritual movement dedicated to bringing greater happiness to humankind by overcoming barriers of race, religion, and culture and by working toward the ideal of a world united in peace and harmony. Supported by followers who live in accordance with Master Okawa's words of enlightened wisdom, Happy Science has grown rapidly since its beginnings in Japan and now extends throughout the world. Today, it has twelve million members around the globe, with faith centers in New York, Los Angeles, San Francisco, Tokyo, London, Sydney, Sao Paulo, and Hong Kong, among many other major cities. Master Okawa speaks at Happy Science centers and travels around the world giving public lectures. Happy Science provides a variety of programs and services to support local communities. These programs include preschools, after-school educational programs for youths, and services for senior citizens and the disabled. Members also participate in social and charitable activities, which in the past have included providing relief aid to earthquake victims in China, New Zealand, and Turkey, and to flood victims in Thailand as well as building schools in Sri Lanka.

Programs and Events

Happy Science faith centers offer regular events, programs, and seminars. Join our meditation sessions, video lectures, study groups, seminars, and book events. Our programs will help you:

- Know the purpose and meaning of life
- Know the true meaning of love and create better relationships
- Learn how to meditate to achieve serenity of mind
- Learn how to overcome life's challenges

...and much more.

International Seminars
Each year, friends from all over the world join our international seminars, held at our faith centers in Japan. Different programs are offered each year and cover a wide variety of topics, including improving relationships, practicing the Eightfold Path to enlightenment, and loving yourself, to name just a few.

Happy Science Monthly
Happy Science regularly publishes various magazines for readers around the world. The Happy Science Monthly, which now spans over 200 issues, contains Master Okawa's latest lectures, words of wisdom, stories of remarkable life-changing experiences, world news, and much more to guide members and their friends to a happier life. This is available in many other languages, including Portuguese, Spanish, French, German, Chinese, and Korean.

Happy Science Basics, on the other hand, is a 'theme-based' booklet made in an easy-to-read style for those new to Happy Science, which is also ideal to give to friends and family.

You can pick up the latest issues from Happy Science, subscribe to have them delivered (see our contacts page) or view them online.*

* Online editions of the *Happy Science Monthly* and *Happy Science Basics* can be viewed at: **info.happy-science.org/category/magazines/**

For more information, visit happy-science.org

CONTACT INFORMATION

Happy Science is a worldwide organization with faith centers around the globe. For a comprehensive list of centers, visit the worldwide directory at http://www.happy-science.org or www.happyscience-na.org. The following are some of the many Happy Science locations:

United States and Canada

New York
79 Franklin Street, New York,
NY 10013, U.S.A.
TEL 1-212-343-7972
FAX 1-212-343-7973
Email: ny@happy-science.org
Website: www.happyscience-ny.org

San Francisco
525 Clinton Street,
Redwood City, CA 94062, U.S.A.
Phone/Fax: 1-650-363-2777
Email: sf@happy-science.org
Website: www.happyscience-sf.org

Los Angeles
1590 E. Del Mar Blvd.,
Pasadena, CA 91106, U.S.A.
Phone: 1-626-395-7775
Fax: 1-626-395-7776
Email: la@happy-science.org
Website: www.happyscience-la.org

Atlanta
1874 Piedmont Ave. , NE
Suite 360-C Atlanta, GA 30324,
U.S.A.
Phone/Fax: 1-404-892-7770
Email: atlanta@happy-science.org
Website: www.atlanta.happyscience-na.org

Orange County
10231 Slater Ave #204
Fountain Valley, CA 92708
U.S.A.
Phone: 1-714-745-1140
Email: oc@happy-science.org

Florida
5208 8th Street,
Zephyrhills, FL 33542 U.S.A.
Phone:1-715-0000
Fax: 1-813-715-0010
Email: florida@happy-science.org
Website: www.happyscience-fl.org

New Jersey
725 River Road, #102B
Edgewater, NJ 07020 U.S.A.
Phone: 1-201-313-0127
Fax: 1-201-313-0120
Email: nj@happy-science.org
Website: www.happyscience-nj.org

Hawaii (Oahu)
1221 Kapiolani Blvd., Suite 920
Honolulu, HI 96814, U.S.A.
Phone: 1-808-591-9772
Fax: 1-808-591-9776
Email: hi@happy-science.org
Website: www.happyscience-hi.org

Hawaii (Kauai)
4504 Kukui Street
Dragon Building Suite 21
Kapaa, HI 96746 U.S.A.
Phone: 1-808-822-7007
Fax: 1-808-822-6007
Email: kauai-hi@happy-science.org
Website: www.happyscience-kauai.org

San Diego
7841 Balboa Avenue, Suite #202,
San Diego, CA 92111 U.S.A.
Phone: 1-626-395-7775
Email: sandiego@happy-science.org

Toronto
323 College Street.,
Toronto ON M5T 1S2, Canada
Phone/Fax: 1-416-901-3747
Email: toronto@happy-science.org
Website: www.happy-science.ca

Vancouver
#212-2609 East 49th Avenue,
Vancouver, BC,V5S 1J9, Canada
Phone: 1-604-437-7735
Fax: 1-604-437-7764
Email: vancouver@happy-science.org
Website: www.happy-science.ca

International

Tokyo
1-6-7 Togoshi, Shinagawa,
Tokyo, 142-0041 Japan
Phone: 81-3-6384-5770
Fax: 81-3-6384-5776
Email: tokyo@happy-science.org
Website: www.happy-science.org

Sydney
516 Pacific Highway, Lane Cove
North, NSW 2066, Australia
Phone: 61-2-9411-2877
Fax: 61-2-9411-2822
Email: sydney@happy-science.org
Website: www.happyscience.org.au

London
3 Margaret Street,
London, W1W 8RE, United Kingdom
Phone: 44-20-7323-9255
Fax: 44-20-7323-9344
Email: eu@happy-science.org
Website: www.happyscience-uk.org

Seoul
74, Sadang-ro27-gil,
Dongjak-gu, Seoul, South Korea
Phone: 82-2-3478-8777
Fax: 82-2-3478-9777
Email: korea@happy-science.org
Website: www.happyscience-korea.org

Taipei
No.89, Lane 155,
Dunhua N. Road.,
Songshan District,
Taipei City 105, Taiwan
Phone: 886-2-2719-9377
Fax: 886-2-2719-5570
Email: taiwan@happy-science.org
Website: www.happyscience-tw.org

Malaysia
No 22A, Block2, Jalil Link
Jalan Jalil Jaya 2, Bukit Jalil
57000, Kuala Lumpur
Malaysia
Phone: 60-3-8998-7877
Fax: 60-3-8998-7977
Email: malaysia@happy-science.org
Website: www.happyscience.org.my

Brazil Headquarters
R. Domingos de Morais 1154,
Vila Mariana, Sao Paulo, SP-CEP
04009-002, Brazil
Phone: 55-11-5088-3800
Fax: 55-11-5088-3806
Email: sp@happy-science.org
Website: www.happyscience-br.org

Jundiai
Rua Congo, 447,
Jd.Bonfiglioli, Jundiai, CEP
13207-340, Brazil
Phone: 55-11-4587-5952
Email:jundiai@happy-science.org

Nepal
Kathmandu Metropolitan City,
Ring Road, Sitapaila,
Kimdol, Ward No.15,
Harati Marg,Kathmandu, Nepal
Phone: 977-1-4272931
Email: nepal@happy-science.org

Uganda
Plot 877 Rubaga Road, Kampala,
P.O. Box 34130, Kampala,
Uganda
Phone: 256-79-3238-002
Email:uganda@happy-science.org
Website: www.happyscience-uganda.org

HAPPINESS REALIZATION PARTY

The Happiness Realization Party (HRP) was founded in May 2009 by Master Ryuho Okawa as part of the Happy Science Group to offer concrete and proactive solutions to the current issues such as military threats from North Korea and China and the long-term economic recession. HRP aims to implement drastic reforms of the Japanese government, thereby bringing peace and prosperity to Japan. To accomplish this, HRP proposes two key policies:

1) Strengthening the national security and the Japan-US alliance which plays a vital role in the stability of Asia.
2) Improving the Japanese economy by implementing drastic tax cuts, taking monetary easing measures and creating new major industries.

HRP advocates that Japan should offer a model of a religious nation that allows diverse values and beliefs to coexist, and that contributes to global peace.

For more information, visit en.hr-party.jp

HAPPY SCIENCE UNIVERSITY

★ This is an unaccredited institution of higher education.

The Founding Spirit and the Goal of Education

Based on the founding philosophy of the university, "Pursuit of happiness and the creation of a new civilization," education, research and studies will be provided to help students acquire deep understanding grounded in religious belief and advanced expertise with the objectives of producing "great talents of virtue" who can contribute in a broad-ranging way to serve Japan and the international society.

Overview of Faculties and Departments

Faculty of Human Happiness, Department of Human Happiness

Students in this faculty will pursue liberal arts from various perspectives with a multidisciplinary approach, explore and envision an ideal state of human beings and society.

Faculty of Successful Management, Department of Successful Management

This faculty aims to realize successful management that helps organizational entities of all kinds to create value and wealth for society and to contribute to the happiness and the development of management and employees as well as society as a whole.

Faculty of Future Industry, Department of Industrial Technology

This faculty aims to nurture engineers who can resolve various issues facing modern civilization from a technological standpoint and contribute to the creation of new industries of the future.

HAPPY SCIENCE ACADEMY JUNIOR AND SENIOR HIGH SCHOOL

Happy Science Academy Junior and Senior High School is a boarding school founded with the goal of educating the future leaders of the world who can have a big vision, persevere, and take on new challenges. Currently, there are two campuses in Japan; the Nasu Main Campus in Tochigi Prefecture, founded in 2010, and the Kansai Campus in Shiga Prefecture, founded in 2013.

ABOUT IRH PRESS USA INC.

IRH Press USA Inc. was founded in 2013 as an affiliated firm of IRH Press Co., Ltd. Based in New York, the press publishes books in various categories including spirituality, religion, and self-improvement and publishes books by Ryuho Okawa, the author of 100 million books sold worldwide. For more information, visit okawabooks.com.

Follow us on:
Facebook: MasterOkawaBooks
Twitter: OkawaBooks
Goodreads: RyuhoOkawa
Instagram: OkawaBooks
Pinterest: OkawaBooks

BOOKS BY RYUHO OKAWA

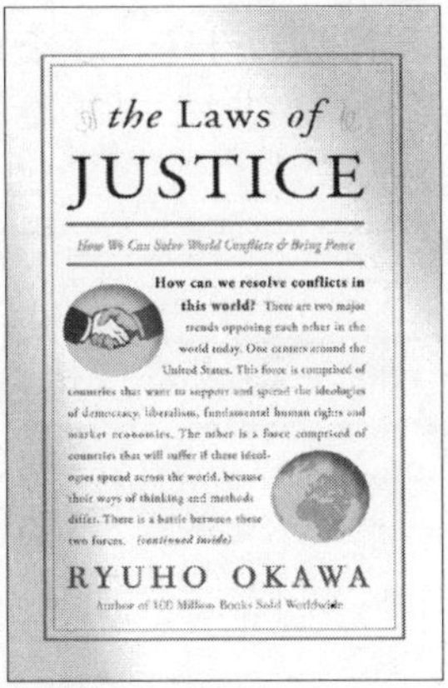

THE LAWS OF JUSTICE

How We Can Solve World Conflicts & Bring Peace

Softcover/208 pages/$15.95/ISBN: 978-1-942125-05-1

How can we solve conflicts in this world? Why is it that we continue to live in a world of turmoil, when we all wish to live in a world of peace and harmony?

In recent years, we've faced issues that jeopardize international peace and security, including the rise of ISIS, Syrian civil war and refugee crisis, break-off of diplomatic relations between Saudi Arabia and Iran, Russia's annexation of Crimea, China's military expansion, and North Korea's nuclear development.

This book shows what global justice is from a comprehensive perspective of the Supreme God. Becoming aware of this view will let us embrace differences in beliefs, recognize other people's divine nature, and love and forgive one another. It will also become the key to solving the issues we face, whether they're religious, political, societal, economic, or academic, and help the world become a better and safer world for all of us living today.

INTO THE STORM OF INTERNATIONAL POLITICS

THE NEW STANDARDS OF THE WORLD ORDER

Ebook/2307KB/$13.99/ISBN: 978-1-941779-31-6

The world is now seeking a new idea or a new philosophy that will show us the direction we should head in. In this book, Okawa presents new standards of the world order while giving his own analysis on world affairs concerning the U.S., China, Islamic State and others.

7 FUTURE PREDICTIONS

SPIRITUAL INTERVIEW WITH
THE GUARDIAN SPIRIT OF HENRY KISSINGER

Ebook/4382KB/$8.99/ISBN: 978-1-943869-12-1

Henry Kissinger is an expert in international politics who served as the U.S. Secretary of State for both Nixon and Ford administrations, promoting reconciliation between the U.S. and China as well as the détente policy between the U.S. and Russia, and who gave significant impact to the world trend since the 1970s. In this book, his guardian spirit (a part of Kissinger's subconscious)makes seven near-future predictions (as of September 2016) including political issues in the U.S. that could occur as a result of the presidential election, as well as the future of the EU, Islamic countries, China and North Korea.

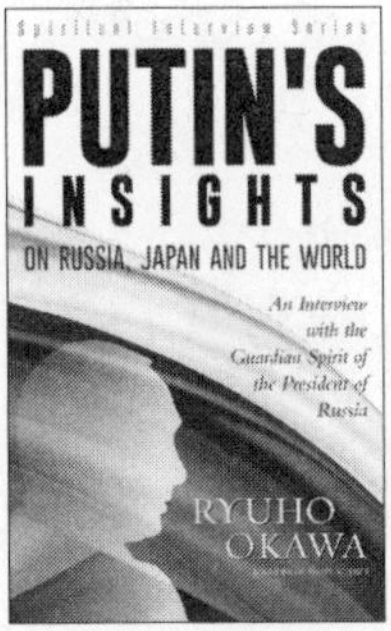

PUTIN'S INSIGHTS ON RUSSIA, JAPAN AND THE WORLD

AN INTERVIEW WITH THE GUARDIAN SPIRIT OF THE PRESIDENT OF RUSSIA

Ebook / 1932KB / $8.99 / ISBN: 978-1-943869-08-4

In this book, Okawa summons the guardian spirit of President Putin and asks his opinion on the current world leaders, how he looks upon Syrian affairs and the confusion in the EU, and on what he predicts will happen in the next 5 years with the Asian crisis.

SAMURAI PRESIDENT OF THE PHILIPPINES

SPIRITUAL INTERVIEW WITH THE GUARDIAN SPIRIT OF RODRIGO DUTERTE

Ebook / 4004KB / $8.99 / ISBN: 978-1-943869-14-5

Samurai President of the Philippines contains the spiritual interview with the subconscious of President Duterte, and reveals that the president is the reincarnation of the internationally renowned, proud Japanese military officer. The secret to his hard-lined leadership of executing over one thousand drug offenders lies in his past life as a Japanese general who fought a deadly battle. Here is the nature of his soul and the true mind of the "samurai president" who will be a key person in Asia from now on.

HAVE FAITH IN GREAT AMERICA LIBERTY AND WORLD JUSTICE FOR ALL:

PRESIDENT OBAMA'S WEAK AMERICA COULD TRIGGER A GLOBAL CRISIS

Ebook/367KB/$13.99/ISBN: 978-1-937673-23-9

Have Faith in Great America: Liberty and World Justice for All is Okawa's earnest message to the United States of America. The world's future depends on America's fulfillment of its long-held sacred mission of protecting the faith, liberty, and justice of people and nations around the world, and on the development of strong bonds between the United States and Japan.

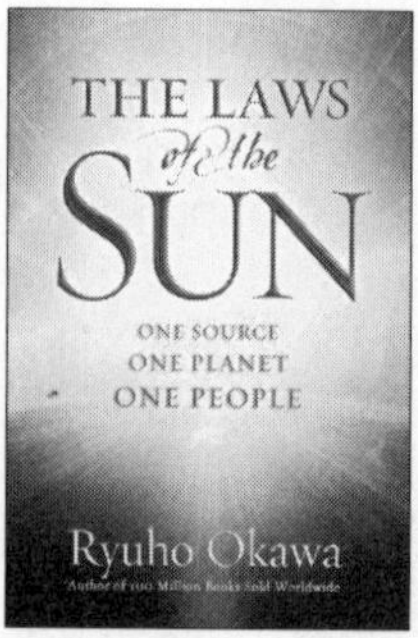

THE LAWS OF THE SUN

ONE SOURCE, ONE PLANET, ONE PEOPLE

Hardcover/264 pages/$24.95/ISBN: 978-1-937673-04-8

Imagine if you could ask God why He created this world and what spiritual laws He used to shape us—and everything around us. In *The Laws of the Sun*, Okawa outlines these laws of the universe and provides a road map for living one's life with greater purpose and meaning. This powerful book shows the way to realize true happiness—a happiness that continues from this world through the other.

THE NINE DIMENSIONS
UNVEILING THE LAWS OF ETERNITY

A LIFE OF TRIUMPH
UNLEASHING YOUR LIGHT UPON THE WORLD

THE MIRACLE OF MEDITATION
OPENING YOUR LIFE TO PEACE, JOY, AND THE POWER WITHIN

THE ESSENCE OF BUDDHA
THE PATH TO ENLIGHTENMENT

THINK BIG!
BE POSITIVE AND BE BRAVE TO ACHIEVE YOUR DREAMS

THE HEART OF WORK
10 KEYS TO LIVING YOUR CALLING

INVITATION TO HAPPINESS
7 INSPIRATIONS FROM YOUR INNER ANGEL

MESSAGES FROM HEAVEN
WHAT JESUS, BUDDHA, MUHAMMAD, AND MOSES WOULD SAY TODAY

THE MOMENT OF TRUTH
BECOME A LIVING ANGEL TODAY

SECRETS OF THE EVERLASTING TRUTHS
A NEW PARADIGM FOR LIVING ON EARTH

CHANGE YOUR LIFE, CHANGE THE WORLD
A SPIRITUAL GUIDE TO LIVING NOW

For a complete list of books, visit okawabooks.com

MOVIES

Master Okawa is the creator and executive producer of ten films. These movies have received various awards and recognition around the world.

Movie Titles :

- The Terrifying Revelations of Nostradamus (1994)
- Love Blows Like the Wind (1997)
- The Laws of the Sun (2000)
- The Golden Laws (2003)
- The Laws of Eternity (2006)
- The Rebirth of Buddha (2009)
- The Final Judgement (2012)
- The Mystical Laws (2012)
- The Laws of the Universe - Part 0 (2015)
- I'm Fine, My Angel (2016)

THE MYSTICAL LAWS

The winner of

"2013 Remi Special Jury Award"

for Theatrical Feature Productions in WorldFest Houston International Film Festival

Other Awards:

- "Palm Beach International Film Festival" Nominated for Best Feature Official Selection
- "Asian Film Festival of Dallas" Official selection
- "Proctors 4th Annual Animation Festival" Official Selection
- "Buddhist Film Festival Europe" Official Selection
- "Japan-Filmfest Hamburg" Official Selection
- "Monstra,the Lisbon Animated Film Festival" Official Selection

Now available on *Video On Demand*, visit *mystical-laws.com*

For more information, visit hspicturesstudio.com